PRAYERS OF
POPE JOHN PAUL II

Edited by
John F. McDonald

Foreword by
Bishop Agnellus Andrew

 St Paul Publications

St Paul Publications
Middlegreen, Slough SL3 6BT, England

Copyright © St Paul Publications 1982
First published March 1982
Printed by the Society of St Paul, Slough
ISBN 0 85439 214 9

St Paul Publications is an activity of the priests and brothers of the Society of St Paul who promote the Christian message through the mass media.

CONTENTS

	Page
Editor's note	7
Foreword by Bishop Agnellus Andrew	9
For his Papal ministry	13
To God the Father	15
To the Christ Child	16
To Christ the Redeemer	18
To Christ in the Eucharist	21
To the Holy Spirit	24
On the feast of the Immaculate Conception	29
At the Shrine of the Immaculate Conception	37
To the Virgin of Guadalupe	39
At Jasna Gora	41
At Belém do Para, Brazil	43
At Frascati	45
At the close of the month of May	46
In the Chapel of the Miraculous Medal	47
To the Virgin of Altötting	50
For the Church in Africa	53
For the peoples of Asia	55
For the people and the Church of Brazil	56
For Catholics in the Congo	59
For Ireland	61
For Italy and Europe	64
For the Church of Japan	66
For Mexico and Latin America	68
For Poland	71
For the Church in Zaïre	73
For the past missionaries to Zaïre	74
At the tomb of St Albert the Great	76
To Saints Cyril and Methodius	78
At the tomb of St Francis of Assisi	79
On the feast of St Joseph	80
On the feast of Saints Peter and Paul	81
To St Stanislaus Patron of Poland	82
To the most recent 'Beati'	83
For the family	84

For peace   85
For consolation   87
For Christian unity   88
For vocations   91
For workers   94
For those working with the mass media   95
For the dead   96
To the Merciful Love   97
Glory to Christ the Word of God   98
Various   99

Index   105

EDITOR'S NOTE

We are grateful to Fr Lambert Greenan, O.P., the editor of the English language weekly edition of the *Osservatore Romano,* for his kind permission to use that translation of the prayers contained in this book.

Where the prayers concern a specific subject or intention, e.g., Peace, Christian Unity, Vocations, it has been possible to group them together. In other cases it has not been possible to isolate the various intentions without affecting the structure of the prayer in question. This accounts for the additional references to certain subjects in the index.

John F. McDonald
Rome

FOREWORD

By Bishop Agnellus Andrew, OFM

Pope John Paul II begins every day with several hours of prayer, ending with Mass, in his private chapel. On one wonderful occasion, late in October 1979, I was given the privilege of concelebrating Mass with him.

I remember opening the door and moving into the little chapel. There before the altar was the Pope kneeling at prayer alone, recollected and still. In fact, my impression was of the complete stillness which surrounded him, and later as he celebrated Mass this impression of total quiet and stillness continued. I have seen him many times since on every kind of occasion and wherever he goes, even in the midst of great crowds, he seems to take this air of stillness, and quiet, and prayer with him. I have been told that even when he is driving in his 'Popemobile', with the crowds wildly enthusiastic on all sides, the Pope stands with smiling eyes and arms outstretched, but if you look closely you may see his lips moving in prayer. Clearly he has this supreme gift of building a life of immense apostolic and pastoral activity on the secure foundation of a sense of God's presence and of constant stillness and prayer.

I have often remarked on how two of the most active apostolates in the Church were put under the patronage of two contemplatives. St Therese of Lisieux is the patron of the foreign missions; and St Clare is the patron of television. Unexpected? Yes, but how wonderfully right and what a reminder to all of us in these days of endless movement and ceaseless activity.

This book of prayers of Pope John Paul II does not contain examples of his private prayer as he faces the day on the prie-dieu in his chapel, or as he commits himself into the loving hands of God last thing at night. All these prayers are from the public prayers of the Pope as he meets his people on his pastoral visits to Ireland, or Brazil, or Africa: as he addresses them standing before the statue of Our Blessed Lady in the Piazza di Spagna on the Feast of the Immaculate Conception, or as he prays at the Shrine of Knock in the west of Ireland. In one sense they are very unusual prayers. They do not express merely the deep devotional life of the Holy Father but they are full of teaching, of narration, even of history, always related to the occasion when they were spoken. And they are very often, whatever the occasion, addressed to Our Blessed Lady. Here is an example from the visit to Brazil: 'O Mother! Let this Church following the example of Christ by serving man constantly, defend everyone, especially the poor and the needy, those living on the fringes of society and in want. Let the Church of Brazil always be at the service of justice among men and at the same time contribute to the common good of all and to social peace.

O Mother! Open the hearts of men and let everyone understand that only in the spirit of the Gospel and observing the commandment of love and the beatitudes of the Sermon on the Mount will it be possible to construct a more human world, in which the dignity of all men will really be given new value.

O Mother! Let the Church, which in this land of Brazil has carried out a great work of evangelisation in the past and whose history is rich in experience, accomplish her tasks today with new zeal, with new love of the mission received from Christ.'

And this is from the Pope's Irish visit: 'We entrust to your motherly care the land of Ireland, where you have been and are so much loved. Help this land to stay true to you and your Son always. May prosperity never cause Irish men and women to forget God or abandon their faith. Keep them faithful in prosperity to the faith they would not surrender in poverty and persecution. Save them from greed, from envy, from seeking selfish or sectional interest. Help them to work together with a sense of Christian purpose and a common Christian goal, to build a just and peaceful and loving society where the poor are never neglected and the rights of all, especially the weak, are respected. Queen of Ireland, Mary, Mother of the heavenly and earthly Church, Máthair Dé, keep Ireland true to her spiritual tradition and her Christian heritage.'

This book is timely. One of the unexpected developments over the past twenty years has been a great renewal of prayer, especially in the lives of the young. It expresses itself in a wide variety of ways: in the Charismatic Movement on the one hand, and in pop songs and plays, and dance, and mimes, on the other—all ways of giving glory to God and of expressing their own deep sense of need for communion with him.

This great and wonderful Pope responds to this at all times. He is now acknowledged universally as the great spiritual leader in the world today. Time after time in his prayers, in his writings, in his messages to the Church it is transparently clear that his whole life is based on love for Jesus Christ our beloved Saviour and Redeemer and on Mary through whom Jesus came to us and who longs to lead us back to him.

It is not insignificant that the Pope's coat of arms is dominated by a great 'M' for Mary and that he begins every public occasion with the words: 'Praised be Jesus Christ'.

FOR HIS PAPAL MINISTRY

1. The new successor of Peter in the See of Rome, today makes a fervent humble and trusting prayer: Christ, make me become and remain the servant of your unique power, the servant of your sweet power, the servant of your power that knows no eventide. Make me be a servant. Indeed, the servant of your servants.

(22.10.78—OR, 2.11.78)

2. To you, O Queen of Martyrs and Mother of the Church, I wish to entrust in a special way this papal ministry of mine and its many-sided significance. It is from the blood of martyrs that, from the very beginning, the Church of your Son was born and grew strong, the Church of Jesus Christ, with whose sacrifice on the cross you, Mother, cooperate with the maternal sacrifice of your heart (cf. Lumen Gentium, 58).

Many indeed are the examples we find of such witness borne by the holy and blessed martyrs in various parts of the great continent of Asia. The foundation of faith sealed with blood seems already deeply rooted in the soil of history. But it is not ourselves, we human beings, who can measure and say whether this is the sufficient foundation for the building up of the service of the Gospel and of the Church in these vast areas of land and on the countless surrounding islands. The judgement of this we leave to the mercy of God himself, to the heart of our Redeemer and Lord, and to the Holy Spirit who guides humanity and the Church through the testimony of blood towards the kingdom of love and truth.

And yet, all this immense work that is ever before us, I, John Paul II, with the full consciousness of my human weakness and unworthiness, desire—as I always do—to entrust to you, Mother of Christ and of the Church, who

with your ceaseless maternal love watch over her everywhere, ready to serve with every form of help in every
human heart and in the midst of all peoples. And especially
among those who are most sorely tried by suffering, by
poverty and by every sort of affliction whatsoever . . .

Mother of Perpetual Help, accept this humble dedication
and place it in the heart of your Son—you, who when you
stood beneath his cross on Calvary were given to each
of us as our Mother.   Amen.

(Baclaran, Philippines,
17.2.81—OR, 23.2.81)

TO GOD THE FATHER

3. Lord, with the faith you have given us, we acknowledge
that you are God almighty, our Creator and provident
Father, the God of hope, in Jesus Christ our Saviour,
the God of love in the Holy Spirit our Comforter!

Lord, trusting in your promises which do not pass away,
we want to come always to you, and to find in you relief
in our suffering. However, disciples of Jesus as we are, let
not our will, but yours be done throughout our whole life!

Lord, grateful for Christ's preference for the lepers who
had the good fortune to come into contact with him, seeing
ourselves in them . . . we also thank you for the favours
we receive in everything that helps us, give us relief, and
console us. We thank you for the medicine and for the
doctors, for the care of the nurses, for the circumstances of
life, for those who console us and who are consoled by us,
for those who understand us and accept us, and for the
others.

Lord, grant us patience, serenity, and courage; grant
that we may live a joyful charity, for love of you, towards
those who are suffering more than we and towards those who
though not suffering, have not grasped the meaning of life.

Lord, we ask that our life be useful, we want to serve:
to praise, to give thanks, to atone and to implore with
Christ, for those who worship you and for those who do
not worship you in the world, and for the Church,
scattered all over the earth.

Lord, through the infinite merits of Christ on the cross,
a "Suffering Servant" and our brother with whom we
unite, we pray to you for our families, our friends and
benefactors, for the successful outcome of the Pope's visit,
and for Brazil.   Amen.

(At the Marituba Leper Colony
in Belém, Brazil,
8.7.80—OR, 11.8.80)

15

TO THE CHRIST CHILD

4. Emmanuel! You are in our midst. *You are with us.*
Coming down to the uttermost consequences of that
Covenant made from the beginning with man, and in spite
of the fact that it was violated and broken so many times . . .

You are with us! *Emmanuel!* In a way that really
surpasses everything that man could have thought of you.
You are with us as *Man.*

You are wonderful, truly wonderful, O God, Creator
and Lord of the universe, God with the Father Almighty!
The Logos! The only Son.

God of power! You are with us as man, as a *newborn*
baby of the human race, *absolutely* weak, wrapped in
swaddling clothes and placed in a manger, "because there
was no place for them" in any inn (Lk 2 : 7).

Wonderful! Messenger of Great Counsel!

Is it not precisely because you became man in this way,
came into the world in this way, without a roof to shelter
you, that you became *nearest to man?*

Is it not precisely because you yourself, the newborn
Jesus, are without a roof that you are nearest to those
brothers and sisters of ours in Southern Italy who *have lost
their homes* through the terrible earthquake? And the
people who really come to their aid are precisely the ones
who have you in their hearts, you who were born in
Bethlehem without a home.

Is it not precisely because from the first days of your
life you were *threatened* with death at the hands of Herod
that you are particularly close, the closest, to those who are
threatened in any way, those who die at the hands of
murderers, those who are denied basic human rights?

And still more: is it not for this reason that you are
closer to those whose life is already threatened in their
mother's womb?

O truly wonderful! The God of power in his weakness
as a child.

From all the parts of Rome and of the world we are setting out towards you. We are being drawn by your birth at Bethlehem. Could you have done anything more than you have done in order to be Emmanuel, God with us? Anything *more than what our amazed eyes behold*: the eyes of the people of the different parts of the world, the different countries and continents, the different parts of every geographical longitude and latitude, in the same way as once the eyes of Mary, of Joseph, and then the eyes of the Shepherds and of the Wise Men from the East beheld!

Truly *blessed are the eyes* that see what you see!

You are the Prince of Peace! Peace: what a great good it is for people! How much it is desired in the modern world, and at the same time how much it is threatened.

You are *Father for ever*. Man who grows from his many-sided past, faces the future, and at the same time worries about his own future, about the future of the world. Christ, may you be the future of man!

Isaiah said that upon your shoulders "dominion rests" (9:5). What is this dominion upon your shoulders, weak Child, what is this dominion?

We know what it is. You have enabled us to know it completely, *from the manger to the Cross*, from Bethlehem to Calvary, from your birth to your resurrection.

It is not dominion "over man". It is dominion "for man". It is the *power of the redemption*. It is truth and love.

Behold, you are born at Bethlehem, that in you may be revealed that love with which the Father has so loved the world as to give his only-begotten Son ... (cf. Jn 3:16).

At this moment we are all spiritually present at the place where you were born. We gaze at you, O Newborn one: we gaze from Rome and from the world.

Blessed are the *eyes that see what we see*!

"A child is born to us, a Son is given to us." Yes! A Son has been given to us. In this Son we are all *once more given back to ourselves*! He is our blessing.

(From the "Urbi et Orbi" Message,
25.12.80—OR, 29.12.80)

B

TO CHRIST THE REDEEMER

5. Jesus Christ, we are about to conclude this holy day of Good Friday at the foot of your cross. Just as once in Jerusalem at the foot of the cross there stood your Mother, John, Mary Magdalen and the other women, so do we stand here. We are deeply moved by the importance of the moment. We cannot find the words to express all that our hearts feel. This evening, when—after you had been taken down from the cross they laid you in a tomb at the foot of Calvary— we wish to ask you *to stay with us through your cross;* you, who through the cross took leave of us. We ask you to stay with the Church: to stay with humanity; not to be dismayed if many, perhaps, pass by your cross with indifference, if some go away from it, and others do not reach it.

And yet, perhaps, never so much as today has man had need of this power and this wisdom that you yourself are, you alone: through your cross!

So stay with us in this deep mystery of your death, in which you revealed how much "God loved the world" (Jn 3 : 16). Stay with us and draw us yourself (cf. Jn 13 : 32), you who fell beneath this cross. Stay with us through your Mother, to whom from the cross, you especially entrusted every human being (cf. Jn 19 : 27).

Stay with us!

Stat Crux, dum volvitur orbis! Yes, "the Cross stands high upon the world as it goes round!"

(Colosseum, Rome, Good Friday,
1979—OR, 17.4.79)

6. Let us cry out and pray with Christ:
"Father, forgive them; for they know not what they do" (Lk 23 : 34).
"My God, my God, why hast thou forsaken me?" (Mt 27 : 46).

"Father, into thy hands I commend my spirit"
(Lk 23 : 46).

Let us cry out and pray as though echoing these words
of Christ:

Father, accept us all in the cross of Christ; accept the
Church and humanity, the Church and the world.

Accept those who accept the cross; those who do not
understand it and those who avoid it; those who do not
accept it and those who fight it in order to erase and uproot
this sign from the land of the living.

Father, accept us all in the cross of your Son!

Accept each of us in the cross of Christ!

Disregarding everything that happens in man's heart,
disregarding the fruits of his works and of the events of
the modern world, accept man!

May the cross of your Son remain as the sign of the
acceptance of the prodigal son by the Father.

May it remain as the sign of the Covenant, of the new
and eternal Covenant.

(Colosseum, Rome, Good Friday,
1980—OR, 14.4.80)

7. And behold: we, who at the end of Good Friday in Rome
are standing near the Colosseum, beneath the cross of the
ages, wish, through your cross and passion, O Christ,
to cry out today that mercy that has irreversibly entered
into the history of man, into our whole human history—
and which in spite of the appearances of weakness is stronger
than evil. It is the greatest power and force upon which
man can sustain himself, threatened as he is from so many
sides.

Holy is God,

Holy and strong,

Holy immortal one, have mercy on us.

Have mercy: eleison: miserere!

May the power of your love once more be shown to be
greater than the evil that threatens it. May it be shown
to be *greater than sin*—than the many sins—that in an ever

19

more absolute form claim the public right of citizenship in the lives of people and of societies.

May the power of your cross, O Christ, be shown to be *greater than the author of sin,* who is called "the prince of this world" (Jn 12 : 31).

For by your blood and your passion you have *redeemed the world*!   Amen.

(Colosseum, Rome, Good Friday, 1981—OR, 27.4.81)

TO CHRIST IN THE EUCHARIST

8. Christ in the Eucharist, accept this expression of adoration and love which the Church renders to you *by means of the ministry of the Bishop of Rome,* Peter's successor. Be worshipped through the memory of all my predecessors who worshipped you before the eyes of Rome and of the world.

At the end of today's liturgy, let your holy Mother who gave you, Eternal Son of the Father, a human body receive you from our hands in the court of her temple:

Hail, O true Body, born of the Virgin Mary, which really suffered and was sacrificed on the cross for mankind; may you be foretasted by us when the test of death arrives! Amen.

(Rome, Feast of Corpus Christi,
1979—OR, 25.6.79)

9. O Christ the Saviour, we give you thanks for your redeeming sacrifice, the only hope of men!

O Christ the Saviour, we give you thanks for the eucharistic breaking of Bread, which you instituted in order to really meet your brothers, in the course of the centuries!

O Christ the Saviour, put into the hearts of the baptized the desire to offer themselves with you and to commit themselves for the salvation of their brothers!

You who are really present in the Blessed Sacrament, spread your blessings abundantly on your people gathered in Lourdes, in order that this Congress may truly remain a sign of the "new world". Amen.

(Eucharistic Congress at Lourdes,
July, 1981—OR, 27.7.81)

10. "Lord stay with us".

These words were spoken for the first time by the disciples of Emmaus. Subsequently in the course of the centuries they have been spoken, an infinite number of times, by the lips of so many of your disciples and confessors, O Christ.

As Bishop of Rome and first servant of this temple, which stands on the place of St Peter's martyrdom, I speak the same words today.

I speak them to invite you, Christ, in your Eucharistic presence to accept the daily adoration continuing through the entire day, in this temple, in this basilica, in this chapel.

Stay with us today and stay, from now on, every day, according to the desire of my heart, which accepts the appeal of so many hearts from various parts, sometimes far away, and above all meets the desire of so many inhabitants of this Apostolic See.

Stay! That we may meet you in the prayer of adoration and thanksgiving, in the prayer of expiation and petition, to which all those who visit this basilica are invited.

Stay! You who are at one and the same time veiled in the Eucharistic mystery of faith and are also revealed under the species of bread and wine, which you have assumed in this Sacrament.

Stay! That your presence in this temple may incessantly be reconfirmed, and that all those who enter here may become aware that it is your house, "the dwelling of God with men" (Rev 21 : 3) and, visiting this basilica, may find in it the very source of life and holiness that gushes from your Eucharistic Heart.

We begin this perpetual, daily adoration of the Blessed Sacrament at the beginning of Advent in the Year of the Lord 1981, a year in which we have celebrated jubilees and anniversaries important for the Church, a year of important events.

The Eucharist is the sacramental testimony of your first Coming, with which the words of the prophets were reconfirmed and expectations were fulfilled. You have left us, O Lord, your Body and your Blood under the species of bread and wine that they may bear witness to the fact that the world has been redeemed—that through them your Paschal Mystery may reach all men as the Sacrament of life and salvation. The Eucharist is at the same time a constant announcement of your Second Coming and the sign of the definitive Advent and also of the expectation of the whole Church.

"When we eat this bread and drink this cup, we proclaim your death, Lord Jesus, until you come in glory".

Every day and every hour we wish to adore you, stripped under the species of bread and wine, to renew the hope of the "call to glory" (cf. 1 Pet 5 : 10), the beginning of which you constituted with your glorified body "at the Father's right hand".

One day, O Lord, you asked Peter: "Do you love me?"

You asked him three times—and three times the Apostle answered: "Lord, you know everything: you know that I love you" (Jn 21 : 15-17).

May the answer of Peter, on whose tomb this basilica was erected, be expressed by this daily and day-long adoration which we have begun today.

May the unworthy successor of Peter in the Roman See —and all those who take part in the adoration of your Eucharistic Presence—attest with every visit of theirs and make ring out again the truth contained in the Apostle's words:

"Lord you know everything; you know that I love you". Amen.

(St Peter's Basilica, Rome,
2.12.81—OR, 14.12.81)

TO THE HOLY SPIRIT

11. "O most blessed Light divine,
      Shine within these hearts of yours,
      And our inmost being fill!" (Sequence for Pentecost)
      Fill these hearts in our times, in which the face of the
earth has been so enriched thanks to man's creativity and
labour through the works of science and technology, when
there has been so profound an exploration of the interior
of the earth and of the spaces of the universe, and when
at the same time mankind finds itself face to face with
previous unknown menaces from forces that man himself
has released.

      Today, we, the pastors of the Church, heirs of those
who received the Holy Spirit in the Upper Room of
Pentecost, must go forth as they did, conscious of the
immensity of the Gift that is given in the Church to the
human family. We must go forth, continually go forth into
the world and, in the different places on earth where we are,
we must repeat with still greater fervour:

      "Let your Spirit descend and renew the face of the
earth."

      Let him descend.

      Throughout the history of mankind, throughout the
history of the visible world, the Church does not cease
to confess:

      "We believe in the Spirit."

      "We believe in the Holy Spirit, the Lord, the giver of
life."

      "Credo in Spiritum Sanctum, Dominum et vivificantem."
In this Spirit we remain.   Amen.

(Homily in St Peter's, Feast of Pentecost,
1981—OR, 15.6.81)

12. Let us thank the Holy Spirit for the day of Pentecost! Let
us thank him for the birth of the Church! Let us thank

him because at that birth was present the Mother of Christ, who persevered in prayer with the first community!

Let us give thanks for the Motherhood of Mary, which was communicated to the Church and continues to be so! Let us give thanks for the Mother who is ever present in the Upper Room of Pentecost!

Let us give thanks because we can also call her the Mother of the Church!

You, who more than any other human being were entrusted to the Holy Spirit, help your Son's Church to persevere in the same dedication, that she may be able to pour out upon all people the indescribable benefits of redemption and sanctification, for the setting free of the whole creation (cf. Rom 8:21).

You, who were with the Church at the beginning of her mission, intercede for her, that as she goes into all the world she may continually teach all nations and proclaim the Gospel to every creature. May the word of Divine Truth and the Spirit of Love find entry into people's hearts, because without this Truth and this Love, they cannot really live the fullness of life.

You, who in the fullest way knew the power of the Holy Spirit, when it was granted to you to conceive in your virginal womb the eternal Word and bring him into the world, obtain for the Church the gift of being able continually to bring forth through water and the Holy Spirit the sons and daughters of the whole human family, without any distinction of language, race and culture, thus giving them the "power to become children of God" (Jn 1:12).

You, who are in such a profound and maternal way linked to the Church, by preceding along the paths of faith, hope and love the whole people of God, embrace all those who are on pilgrimage through the temporal life towards their eternal destiny, and do so with that love which the divine Redeemer himself, your Son, poured into your heart as he hung on the cross. Be the Mother of all our earthly journeyings, however tortuous they may become, so that we may all meet again at last in that great community that your Son has called the flock, and offered for it his own life as the Good Shepherd.

You, who are the first handmaid of the unity of Christ's Body, help us, help all the faithful who feel so keenly the tragedy of the historical divisions of Christianity, to seek persistently the path to the perfect unity of the Body of Christ through unreserved fidelity to the Spirit of Truth and Love granted to them at the price of the cross and death of your Son.

You, who ever desired to serve! You who serve as the Mother of the whole family of the children of God, obtain for the Church that, being enriched by the Holy Spirit with the fullness of the hierarchical and charismatic gift, she may go on with constancy towards the future along the path of that renewal that comes from what the Holy Spirit says and which has found expression in the teaching of the Second Vatican Council, that she may take up, in this work of renewal, everything that is true and good, without allowing herself to be deceived in either one direction or the other, but by discerning assiduously among the signs of the times what serves the coming of the Kingdom of God.

Mother of all individuals and peoples, you know all their sufferings and hopes. In your motherly heart you feel all the struggles between good and evil, between light and darkness, that convulse the world: accept the plea which we make in the Holy Spirit directly to your heart, and embrace with the love of the Mother and Handmaid of the Lord those who most await this embrace, and also those whose act of dedication you too await in a particular way. Take under your motherly protection the whole human family, which with affectionate love we entrust to you, O Mother. May there dawn for everyone the time of peace and freedom, the time of truth, of justice and of hope.

You, who through the mystery of your particular sanctity, which was free from all stain from the moment of your conception, feel in a particularly profound way that "the whole creation has been groaning in travail until now" (Rom 8 : 22), while, being "subject to futility", it waits with eager longing to "be set free from its bondage to decay" (Rom 8 : 20-21), you ceaselessly contribute to "the revealing of the sons of God", which "creation awaits with eager longing" (Rom 8:19), in order to enter into the freedom of their glory (cf. Rom 8:21).

O Mother of Jesus, now glorified in heaven, in both body and soul, as the image and beginning of the Church that is to have its completion in the future age—here on earth, until the coming of the day of the Lord (cf. 2 Pet 3:10) do not cease to shine before the pilgrim people of God as a sign of sure hope and consolation (cf. Lumen Gentium, 68).

God the Holy Spirit! who with the Father and the Son are adored and glorified! Accept these words of humble dedication addressed to you in the heart of Mary of Nazareth, your Spouse and the Mother of the Redeemer, whom the Church too calls Mother, for since the Upper Room of Pentecost the Church learns from her her own vocation as a mother! Accept these words of the pilgrim Church, uttered amid labours and joys, amid fears and hopes, words that are the expression of humble and trusting dedication, words with which the Church which was entrusted to you, the Spirit of the Father and Son, in the Upper Room at Pentecost for ever, does not cease to repeat together with you to her divine Spouse: Come! The Spirit and the bride say to the Lord Jesus "Come" (cf. Rev 22:17). Hence the universal Church is seen to be "a people brought into unity from the unity of the Father, the Son and the Holy Spirit" (Lumen Gentium, 4).

And so today we repeat: "Come", placing our trust in your motherly intercession, O clement, O loving, O sweet Virgin Mary.

(St Mary Major's, Feast of Pentecost, 1981—OR, 15.6.81). See also No. 17.

13. Mother, we ask through your intercession, like the disciples in the Upper Room, for the continual assistance of the Holy Spirit and the docility to accept him in the Church; we ask this for those who seek God's truth and for those who must serve it and live it. May Christ always be the "light of the world" (cf. Jn 8:12) and may the world recognize us as his disciples because we remain in his Word and know the truth that will make us free with the freedom of the Sons of God (cf. Jn 8 : 32).

(Homily at Belém, Brazil,
8.7.80—OR, 11.8.80)

ON THE FEAST OF THE IMMACULATE CONCEPTION

14. Ave!

Today we come to greet you, Mary, chosen to be the Mother of the Eternal Word.

We come to this place, guided by a special tradition, and we say to you: Hail, blessed art thou, full of grace ("Ave Maria, gratia plena").

We use the words spoken by Gabriel, the messenger of the Holy Trinity.

We use these words spoken by all generations of the people of God, which has been making its pilgrimage on this earth for nearly two thousand years. We use these words dictated by our hearts: "Ave Maria, gratia plena": full of grace. We come today, on the day when the Church recalls, with the greatest veneration, the fullness of this grace, which God showered upon you from the first moment of your conception.

The Apostle's words fill us with joy: "Where sin increased, grace abounded all the more" (Rom 5: 20).

We rejoice in this special abundance of divine grace in you, who bear the name *Immaculate Conception*.

Today it is particularly we Romans, the inhabitants of this city, which Divine Providence has chosen to be the See of Peter and of his successors, who come to this place. We have been coming in large numbers since Pius XII began this act of filial homage, almost a century after Pius IX blessed this monument to Mary Immaculate. We all come, even if we are not all present here physically; we are present, however, in spirit.

Old and young, parents and children, the healthy and the sick, representatives of the various circles and professions, priests and men and women religious, civil authorities of the city of Rome and of the province of Latium, we all consider it a special privilege to be here today together with the Bishop of Rome, beside this Marian Column, to surround you, Mother, with our veneration and our love.

Accept us, just as we are, here beside you at this annual meeting!

Accept us! Look into our hearts! Accept our concerns and our hopes!

Help us, you who are full of grace, to live in grace, to persevere in grace, and, if necessary, to return to the grace of the living God, which is man's greatest and supernatural good.

Prepare us for your Son's coming! *Accept us*! With our everyday problems, our weaknesses and deficiencies, our crises, and personal, family and social shortcomings.

Do not let us lose goodwill! Do not let us lose sincerity of conscience and uprightness of behaviour!

With your prayer, obtain justice for us. Safeguard peace in the whole world!

In a short time we shall all leave this place. We wish, however, to return to our homes with this joyful certainty that you are with us, you, Mary Immaculate, you, chosen for centuries to be Mother of the Redeemer. Be with us. Be with Rome. Be with the Church and with the world. Amen.

(Piazza di Spagna, Rome,
8.12.79—OR, 17.12.79)

15. Mother of Christ!

On the day of the solemnity of your Immaculate Conception we come to this place, now consecrated by a long Roman tradition; to this spot, surrounded by a constant memory of its inhabitants, to express, at your feet, at this commemorative column, our veneration and our love.

We do it *as a Church,* which Providence chose as St Peter's See and connected with his martyrdom and that of St Paul, his fellow apostle, making this Church a particular centre of unity and love for all the Churches in the whole earthly globe.

We do it simultaneously *as a City* which today, as in

past centuries, feels bound to this great tradition of apostolic mission and service.

So we are again at your feet to testify to you once more our veneration and our love, on the day when the Church recalls the mystery of your exceptional election by God.

Our Mother!

In this place we wish at the same time to speak to you —just as one speaks to one's mother—about everything that constitutes the object of our hopes, but also of our concerns; of our joys, but also of our afflictions; of fears and even of great threats.

Are we capable of expressing all that and of calling it by name?

It would take too long, it would be like a long litany of the questions and problems that beset modern man, the nations, mankind, beginning with the beloved Italian land, so hard hit by the recent earthquake. Some news that reaches us from all over the world (wars, acts of violence, terrorism, disasters and cataclysms which leave victims and mourning in so many families) is a cause of particular apprehension. Among the events known to everyone I would like to mention the grievous killings, even of religious persons, such as in Salvador, stained by the blood of fratricidal strife. And I cannot but speak here, as a son of my native country, of my Polish land. Alarming news is circulating and we all hope it will not be confirmed.

I entrust to you, O Immaculate Mother of God, my people, my native country, so faithful to Christ and to the Church, so devoted to you.

Other problems remain in the secrecy of human hearts and consciences. Each of us brings here so many similar concerns and so many problems which concern himself, his family, his own environment, the community with which he is connected or for which he feels responsible.

Even if we do not express it aloud, you, O Mother, know better, because a mother always knows . . .

You, O Mother, know better what are the problems of the Church and of the modern world, with which the Bishop of Rome comes to you today, like each of those present.

So accept them, kindly accept and answer this wordless prayer of ours.

And above all, receive the expressions of our fervent gratitude for your being with us, meeting us every day, and particularly on this solemn day.

And stay!

Be with us more and more. Meet us more and more often, because we need it so much. Speak to us by your motherhood, by your simplicity and holiness. Speak to us by your Immaculate Conception!

Speak to us continually!

And obtain for us the grace—even if we are distant— of not becoming insensitive to your presence in our midst. Amen.

(Piazza di Spagna, Rome, 8.12.80—OR, 15.12.80)

16. Immaculate Mother!

On this solemn day, while we find ourselves before your figure in keeping with the tradition of the city where Peter's See is located, we desire above all to express the love and veneration with which we surround your Immaculate Conception, which is a sign of the advent of God and of human hope.

The times in which we live have a particular need for this sign.

In fact, the world of today—as the last Council teaches —suffers from many imbalances and they are all "a symptom of the deeper dichotomy that is in man himself . . . He is the meeting point of many conflicting forces. In his condition as a created being he is subject to a thousand shortcomings, but feels untrammelled in his inclinations and destined for a higher form of life . . . Worse still, feeble and sinful as he is, he often does the very thing he hates and does not do what he wants.

And so he feels divided, and the result is a host of discords in social life . . ."

The life of many "is blurred by materialism . . ."

Many "look forward to some future earthly paradise where all the desires of their hearts will be fulfilled.

Nor is it unusual to find people who have lost faith in life . . ." (cf. Gaudium et Spes, 10).

This picture drawn over ten years ago by the Council, could be completed with various particulars which show the great threat hanging over man and the world. These particulars are sufficiently known by all those who are gathered here.

Therefore, the times in which we live need you, Immaculate Mother of the Saviour, who for all generations do not cease to be the sign of the advent of God and the sign of human hope.

Pope Pius XII, who, in the horrible times of the Second World War, dedicated the whole of mankind to your Immaculate Heart, found himself before this sign.

He who by divine will today is his successor in the Roman See puts himself before this sign and says:

"O Mother of men and peoples, you know all their sufferings and their hopes, you feel in a motherly way all the struggles between good and evil, between light and darkness, that shake the world—accept our cry addressed in the Holy Spirit directly to your heart and embrace with the love of the Mother and Handmaid of the Lord the people who are most awaiting this embrace, and at the same time the people whose trust you also particularly expect. Take under your motherly protection the whole human family which we entrust to you with affectionate joy, O Mother. May the time of peace and freedom, the time of truth, justice and hope approach for everyone.

Monstra Te esse Matrem!

Show us that you are our Mother, even if we so little deserve this motherly love.

But a mother's love is always greater! In it is manifested the mercy of God himself, which is more powerful than every evil that has taken possession of man's history and his heart.

You who, treading on the serpent's head, embrace the whole world in your Immaculate Heart, show that you are a Mother!

Monstra Te esse Matrem!

Amen.

(Piazza di Spagna, Rome,
8.12.81—OR, 14.12.81)

c

17. O you, who more than any other human being have been
consecrated to the Holy Spirit, help your Son's Church to
persevere in the same consecration, so that she may pour
out upon all men the ineffable benefits of redemption
and of sanctification, for the liberation of the whole of
creation (cf. Rom 8 : 12).

O you, who were with the Church at the beginning of
her mission, intercede for her in order that, going all over
the world, she may continually teach all the nations and
proclaim the Gospel to every creature. May the word of
Divine Truth and the Spirit of Love find an opening in the
hearts of men, who, without this Truth and without this
Love, really cannot live the fullness of life.

O you, who have known in the fullest way the power
of the Holy Spirit, when it was granted to you to conceive
in your virginal womb and to give birth to the Eternal
Word, obtain for the Church that she may continue to give
new birth through water and the Holy Spirit to the sons
and daughters of the whole human family, without any
distinction of language, race, or culture, giving them in this
way the "power to become the children of God" (Jn 1 : 12).

O you, who are so deeply and maternally bound to the
Church, preceding the whole people of God along the ways
of faith, hope and charity, embrace all men who are on the
way, pilgrims through temporal life towards their eternal
destinies, with that love which the divine Redeemer himself,
your Son, poured into your heart from the cross. Be the
Mother of our earthly lives, even when they become
tortuous, in order that we may find ourselves in the end,
in that large community which your Son called the fold,
offering his life for it as the Good Shepherd.

O you, who are the first handmaid of the unity of the
Body of Christ, help us, help all the faithful, who feel so
painfully the drama of the divisions of Christianity, to seek
with constancy the way to the perfect unity of the Body
of Christ by means of unconditional faithfulness to the
Spirit of Truth and Love, which was given to them by
your Son at the cost of the cross and of death.

O you, who have always wished to serve! You who
serve as Mother the whole family of the children of God,
obtain for the Church that, enriched by the Holy Spirit

with the fullness of hierarchial and charismatic gifts, she
may continue with constancy towards the future along
the way of that renewal which comes from what the Holy
Spirit says and which found expression in the teaching of
Vatican II, assuming in this work of renewal everything
that is true and good, without letting herself be deceived
either in one direction or in the other, but discerning
assiduously among the signs of the times what is useful
for the coming of the Kingdom of God.

O Mother of men and of peoples, you know all their
sufferings and their hopes, you feel in a motherly way all
the struggles between good and evil, between the light and
darkness which shakes the world—accept our cry
addressed in the Holy Spirit directly to your heart and
embrace with the love of the Mother and the Handmaid
of the Lord the peoples who await this embrace the most,
and likewise the peoples whose consecration you, too, are
particularly awaiting. Take under your motherly protection
the whole human family which we consecrate to you, with
affectionate rapture, O Mother. May the time of peace and
freedom, the time of truth, justice and hope, approach
for everyone.

O you, who—through the mystery of your particular
holiness, free from all stain from the moment of your
conception—feel in a particularly deep way that "the whole
of creation has been groaning in travail" (Rom 8 : 22),
while, "subjected to futility, it hopes that it will be set
free from its bondage to decay" (Rom 8 : 20-21), you
contribute unceasingly to the "revealing of the sons of God",
for whom "the creation waits with eager longing"
(Rom 8 : 19), to enter the freedom of their joy
(cf. Rom 8 : 21).

O Mother of Jesus, now glorified in heaven in body and
in soul, as the image and the beginning of the Church,
which is to have its fulfilment in the future age—here on
earth, until the day of the Lord comes (cf. 2 Pet 3 : 10),
do not cease to shine before the pilgrim people of God
as a sign of sure hope and consolation (cf. Lumen Gentium,
68).

Holy Spirit of God, who are worshipped and glorified
with the Father and the Son! Accept these words of humble

consecration addressed to you in the heart of Mary of Nazareth, your Bride and the Mother of the Redeemer, whom the Church too calls her Mother, because right from the Upper Room at Pentecost she has learned from her, her own motherly vocation! Accept these words of the pilgrim Church, uttered amid toils and joys, fears and hopes, words which are the expression of humble and confident trust, words which the Church, for ever consecrated to you, Spirit of the Father and of the Son, in the Upper Room at Pentecost, does not cease to repeat together with you to her divine Bridegroom. Come!

"The Spirit and the Bride say to the Lord Jesus 'Come' " (cf. Rev 22:17). "Thus the Church is seen to be a people brought into unity from the unity of the Father, the Son, and the Holy Spirit" (Lumen Gentium, 4).

Thus we repeat today: "Come", trusting in your motherly intercession, O clement, O loving, O sweet Virgin Mary.

(Before the image of Our Lady
"Salus Populi Romani" in the
Basilica of St Mary Major, Rome,
8.12.81—OR, 14.12.81)
See also No. 12

AT THE SHRINE OF THE IMMACULATE CONCEPTION, WASHINGTON, D.C.

18. Today, as I thank you, Mother, for this presence of yours in the midst of the men and women of this land—a presence which has lasted two hundred years—giving a new form to their social and civic lives in the United States, I commend them all to your Immaculate Heart.

With gratitude and joy I recall that you have been honoured as Patroness of the United States, under the title of your Immaculate Conception, since the days of the Sixth Provincial Council of Baltimore in 1846.

I commend to you, Mother of Christ, and I entrust to you the Catholic Church: the bishops, priests, deacons, individual religious and religious institutes, the seminarians, vocations, and the apostolate of the laity in its various aspects.

In a special way I entrust to you the well-being of the Christian families of this country, the innocence of children, the future of the young, the vocation of single men and women. I ask you to communicate to all the women of the United States a deep sharing in the joy that you experienced in your closeness to Jesus Christ, your Son. I ask you to preserve all of them in freedom from sin and evil, like the freedom which was yours in a unique way from the moment of supreme liberation in your Immaculate Conception.

I entrust to you the great work of ecumenism here, in this land, in which those who confess Christ belong to different Churches and communions. I do this in order that the words of Christ's prayer may be fulfilled: "That they may be one". I entrust to you the consciences of men and women and the voice of public opinion, in order that they may not be opposed to the law of God but follow it as the fount of truth and good.

I add to this, Mother, the great cause of justice and peace in the modern world, in order that the force and energy of love may prevail over hatred and destructiveness, and in order that the children of light may not lack concern for the welfare of the whole human family.

Mother, I commend and entrust to you all that goes to make up earthly progress, asking that it should not be one-sided, but that it should create conditions for the full spiritual advancement of individuals, families, communities and nations. I commend to you the poor, the suffering, the sick and the handicapped, the ageing and the dying. I ask you to reconcile those in sin, to heal those in pain, and to uplift those who have lost their hope and joy. Show to those who struggle in doubt the light of Christ your Son.

The bishops of the Church in the United States have chosen your Immaculate Conception as the mystery to hold the patronage over the people of God in this land. May the hope contained in this mystery overcome sin and be shared by all the sons and daughters of America, and also by the whole human family. At a time when the struggle between good and evil, between the prince of darkness and father of lies and evangelical love is growing more acute, may the light of your Immaculate Conception show to all the way to grace and to salvation.   Amen.

(7.10.79—OR, 5.11.79)

TO THE VIRGIN OF GUADALUPE

19. O Immaculate Virgin, Mother of the true God and Mother of the Church! You, who from this place reveal your clemency and your pity to all those who ask for your protection: hear the prayer that we address to you with filial trust, and present it to your Son Jesus, our sole Redeemer.

Mother of mercy, Teacher of hidden and silent sacrifice, to you, who come to meet us sinners, we dedicate on this day all our being and all our love. We also dedicate to you our life, our work, our joys, our infirmities and our sorrows.

Grant peace, justice and prosperity to our peoples; for we entrust to your care all that we have and all that we are, our Lady and Mother.

We wish to be entirely yours and to walk with you along the way of complete faithfulness to Jesus Christ and his Church: hold us always with your loving hand.

Virgin of Guadalupe, Mother of the Americas, we pray to you for all the bishops, that they may lead the faithful along the paths of intense Christian life, of love and humble service to God.

Contemplate this immense harvest, and intercede with the Lord that he may instil a hunger for holiness in the whole people of God, and grant abundant vocations of priests and religious strong in the faith and zealous dispensers of God's mysteries.

Grant to our homes the grace of loving and respecting life in its beginnings, with the same love with which you conceived in your womb the life of the Son of God. Blessed Virgin Mary, Mother of Fair Love, protect our families, so that they may always be united, and bless the upbringing of our children.

Our hope, look upon us with compassion, teach us to go continually to Jesus and, if we fall, help us to rise again, to return to him, by means of the confession of our faults and sins in the sacrament of penance, which gives peace to the soul. We beg you to grant us a great love for all the holy sacraments, which are, as it were, the signs that your Son left us on earth.

Thus, most holy Mother, with the peace of God in our conscience, with our hearts free from evil and hatred, we will be able to bring to all true joy and true peace, which come to us from your Son, our Lord Jesus Christ, who with God the Father and the Holy Spirit, lives and reigns for ever and ever.   Amen.

(Mexico, 27.1.79—OR, 29.1.79)

AT JASNA GORA

20. Today I come to Jasna Gora as the first pilgrim Pope, and I wish to renew the entire heritage of trust, of consecration and of hope that has been accumulated here with such magnaminity by my brothers in the episcopate and my fellow-countrymen.

Therefore, I entrust to you, Mother of the Church, all the problems of this Church, the whole of her mission and of her service, while the second millennium of the history of Christianity on earth is about to draw to a close.

Spouse of the Holy Spirit and Seat of Wisdom, it is to your intercession that we owe the magnificent *vision and the programme of renewal of the Church* in our age that found expression in the teaching of the Second Vatican Council. Grant that we may make this vision and programme the object of our activity, our service, our teaching, our pastoral care, our apostolate—in the same truth, simplicity and fortitude with which the Holy Spirit has made them known through our humble service. Grant that the whole Church may be reborn by drawing from this new fount of the knowledge of her nature and mission, and not from other foreign or poisoned "cisterns" (cf. Jer 8:14).

Mother of the Church, grant that the Church may enjoy freedom and peace in fulfilling her saving mission and that to this end she may become mature with *a new maturity* of faith and inner unity. Help us to overcome opposition and difficulties. Help us to rediscover all the simplicity and dignity of the Christian vocation. Grant that there may be no lack of "labourers in the Lord's vineyard". Sanctify families. Watch over the souls of the young and the hearts of the children. Help us to overcome the great moral threats against the fundamental spheres of life and love. Obtain for us the grace to be continually renewed through all the beauty of witness given to the cross and resurrection of your Son.

How many problems, Mother, should I not present to you by name in this meeting! *I entrust them all to you,* because you know them best and understand them.

I entrust them to you in the place of the great consecration, from which one has a view not only of Poland but of the whole Church in the dimensions of countries and continents.

I who am the first servant of the Church offer the whole Church to you and entrust it to you with immense confidence, Mother.   Amen.

(4.6.79—OR, 11.6.79)

AT BELEM DO PARA, BRAZIL

21. I invite you all to follow, in silent prayer, the prayer that I recite on behalf of all:

—Mary, you said under the inspiration of the Holy Spirit, that the generations would call you blessed. We take up again the song of past generations so that it will not be interrupted, and exalt in you the most radiant being that mankind has offered to God: the human creature in its perfection, created anew in justice and holiness in a peerless beauty which we call "the Immaculate" or "Full of Grace".

—Mother, you are the "New Eve". The Church of your Son, aware of the fact that it is only with "new men" that is possible to evangelize, namely, to bring the Good News to the world to make a "new humanity", beseeches you that through your intercession the newness of the Gospel, the seed of holiness and fruitfulness, may never be lacking among men.

—Mary, we worship the Father because of the prerogatives that shine in you, but we worship him also because you are always for us "the handmaid of the Lord", a little creature. Because you were capable of saying "Fiat", you became the Bride of the Holy Spirit and the Mother of the Son of God.

—Mother who appear in the pages of the Gospel showing Christ to the Shepherds and the Wise Men, ensure that every evangelizer—bishop, priest, man and woman religious, father or mother, youth or child—be possessed by Christ in order to be capable of revealing him to others.

—Mary, hidden in the multitude while your Son works the miraculous signs of the birth of the kingdom of God, and who speak only to tell others to do whatever he says (cf. Jn 2 : 5), help evangelizers to preach not themselves, but Jesus Christ.

—Mother, wrapped in the mystery of your Son, often without being able to understand, but capable of storing everything and pondering it in your heart (Lk 2 : 19 and 51), bring it about that we evangelizers shall always understand that beyond techniques and strategies, preparation and plans, to evangelize is to immerse oneself in the mystery of Christ and to try to communicate something of him to one's brothers.

—Our Lady of genuine humility, who taught us in the prophetic canticle that "God always exalts the humble" (cf. Lk 1 : 52), always help the "simple and the poor" who seek you with their ordinary piety; help the pastors to lead them in the light of truth and at the same time to be strong and understanding when they have to uproot certain elements that are no longer genuine, and purify certain expressions of popular devotion.   Amen.

(8.7.80—OR, 11.8.80)

AT FRASCATI

22. O shining Virgin, hope and dawn of salvation
for the whole world, turn your kind maternal look
upon us all, gathered here to celebrate and
proclaim your glories!

O faithful Virgin, you who have always been
ready and quick to receive, preserve, and
meditate upon the Word of God, also make us,
amid the tragic events of history, know how to
maintain always intact our Christian faith,
a precious treasure handed down to us by the
Fathers!

O powerful Virgin, who with your feet crush the
head of the tempting serpent, make us fulfill,
day after day, our baptismal promises by which
we renounced Satan, his works, and his allurements, and
let us know how to give the world a joyful witness of
Christian hope.

O merciful Virgin, who have always opened your
maternal heart to the call of humanity, at times divided
by indifference and even, unfortunately, by hatred and
war, make us all know how to grow always, according
to the teaching of your Son, in unity and peace, in order
to be worthy children of the only heavenly Father.   Amen.

(Frascati, 8.9.80—OR, 29.9.80)

AT THE CLOSE OF THE MONTH OF MAY 1979

23. This evening we are celebrating the close of the Marian month 1979. But the month of May cannot end; it must continue in our lives, because veneration, love, devotion to Our Lady cannot disappear from our hearts, on the contrary they must grow and be expressed in a testimony of Christian life, modelled on the example of Mary "the name of the beautiful flower which I always invoke, morning and evening", as the poet Dante sings (Paradise XXIII, 88).

O blessed Virgin, Mother of God, Mother of Christ, Mother of the Church, look upon us mercifully at this hour!

Virgo fidelis, faithful Virgin, pray for us! Teach us to believe as you believed! Make our faith in God, in Christ, in the Church, always to be limpid, serene, courageous, strong and generous.

Mater amabilis, Mother worthy of love! Mater pulchrae dilectionis, Mother of fair love, pray for us! Teach us to love God and our brothers, as you loved them: make our love for others to be always patient, kindly, respectful.

Causa nostrae laetitiae, Cause of our joy, pray for us! Teach us to be able to grasp, in faith, the paradox of Christian joy, which springs up and blooms from sorrow, renunciation, and union with your sacrificed Son: make our joy to be always genuine and full, in order to be able to communicate it to all!   Amen.

(At the Lourdes Grotto, Vatican Gardens, 31.5.79—OR, 25.6.79)

IN THE CHAPEL OF THE MIRACULOUS MEDAL

24. Hail Mary, full of grace, the Lord is with thee, blessed art thou among women, and blessed is the fruit of thy womb, Jesus.

Holy Mary, Mother of God, pray for us, sinners, now and at the hour of our death.   Amen.

O Mary, conceived without sin,

Pray for us who have recourse to thee.

This is the prayer which you inspired, O Mary, in St Catherine Labouré, in this very place, one hundred and fifty years ago; and this invocation, now engraved on the medal, is worn and uttered by so many faithful all over the world today.

On this day when the Church celebrates the visit you paid to Elizabeth when the Son of God had already become incarnate in your womb, our first prayer will be to praise you and bless you. You are blessed among all women! Blessed are you who believed! The Almighty worked wonders for you! The wonder of your divine Motherhood! And in view of it, the wonder of your Immaculate Conception! The wonder of your "Fiat"! You were so closely associated with the cross of our Saviour; your heart was pierced by it, beside his heart. And now, in the glory of your Son, you constantly intercede for us, poor sinners. You watch over the Church whose Mother you are. You watch over each of your children. You obtain from God, for us, all these graces which are symbolised by the rays of light which radiate from your open hands. Provided only that we venture to ask you for them, that we approach you with the confidence, the boldness, the simplicity of a child. And it is in this way that you lead us incessantly towards your divine Son.

In this blessed place, I am happy to tell you again myself, today, of the trust, the very deep attachment, with which you have always graced me. "Totus tuus". I come as a pilgrim, after all those who have come to this chapel in the last hundred and fifty years, like the whole Christian people that throngs here every day to tell you its joy, its trust, and its supplication. I come like Blessed Maximilian Kolbe: before his missionary journey in Japan, exactly fifty years ago, he had come here to seek your special support to spread what he then called the "Militia of Mary Immaculate" and to undertake his marvellous work of spiritual renewal, under your patronage, before giving his life for his brothers. Today Christ asks of his Church a great work of spiritual renewal. And I, the humble successor of Peter, come to entrust to you this great work, as I did at Jasna Gora, at Our Lady of Guadalupe, at Knock, at Pompei, at Ephesus, and as I will do at Lourdes next year.

We dedicate to you our strength and our availability to serve the plan of salvation carried out by your Son. We pray to you that, thanks to the Holy Spirit, faith may deepen and grow stronger in the whole Christian people, that communion may triumph over all the deeds of division, that hope may be revived among those who are disheartened. We pray to you especially for this people of France, for the Church which is in France, for its pastors, for the consecrated souls, for the fathers and mothers of families, for children and the young, for men and women of the third age. We pray to you for those who are in particular distress, physical or moral, who experience the temptation of unfaithfulness, who are shaken by doubt in a climate of unbelief, and also for those who are suffering persecution because of their faith. We entrust to you the apostolate of the laity, the ministry of priests, the witness of sisters. We pray to you that the call to the priestly and religious vocation may be widely heard and followed, for the glory of God and the vitality of the Church in this country, and that of the countries which are still waiting for missionary aid.

We commend to you particularly the multitude of the Daughters of Charity, whose Mother House is established in this place and who, in the spirit of their founder St Vincent de Paul and St Louise de Marillac, are so prompt to serve the Church and the poor in all environments and in all countries. We pray to you for those who dwell in this house and who welcome, in the heart of this feverish capital, all the pilgrims who know the price of silence and prayer.

Hail Mary, full of grace, the Lord is with thee, blessed art thou among women, and blessed is the fruit of thy womb Jesus. Holy Mary, Mother of God, pray for us, sinners, now and at the hour of our death.   Amen.

(Paris, 31.5.80—OR, 9.6.80)

TO THE VIRGIN OF ALTOTTING

25. I greet you, Mother of Graces of Altötting!

For some days, my way as a pilgrim has brought me to Germany, a country rich in history, following in the footsteps of Christianity, which had already arrived here in the time of the Romans. St Boniface, Apostle of the Germans, spread the Christian faith successfully among the young populations and sealed his own missionary work with martyrdom.

My pace is rapid, the programme of the pilgrimage is full, and so I am not able to visit all those places where I would have liked to go because of their historical importance and the desire of my heart. There are so many important and outstanding places!

Today, when I have the privilege of stopping for a few hours here at Altötting, I recognize again that the ways of my present pilgrimage are also connected with the profession of faith, which is the main task of Peter and his successors. When I proclaim Christ, the Son of the living God, "God from God", "Light from Light", "One Being with the Father", at that moment I profess with the whole Church that he became man through the Holy Spirit and was born of the Virgin Mary. Your name, Mary, is indissolubly connected with his Name. Your call and your "yes" belong inseparably, therefore, from that moment onwards, to the mystery of the Incarnation.

With the whole Church I profess and proclaim that Jesus Christ in this mystery is the only mediator between God and man: for his incarnation brought to Adam's sons, who are subjected to the power of sin and of death, redemption and justification. At the same time I am deeply convinced that no one has been called to participate so deeply as you, the Mother of the Redeemer, in this immense and extraordinary mystery; and no one is better able than you alone, Mary, to let us penetrate this mystery more easily and clearly, we who announce it and form a part of it.

I have lived for a long time in this certainty of faith.
With this conviction I began right from the beginning on
my pilgrim way as Bishop of that local Church which the
Apostle Peter founded in Rome, and whose particular task
has always been, and still is today, to serve "communio",
that is, the unity in love of the individual local Churches
and of all brothers and sisters in Christ.

With the same certainty I have come here today, before
your shrine at Altötting, Mother of Graces, surrounded by
the veneration and love of so many believers in Germany
and in Austria, as well as in other German-speaking
countries. Allow me to strengthen this conviction again and
to recite this prayer before you.

Here too, O our Mother, I wish to entrust the Church
to you, because you were present in the Upper Room when
the Church openly proclaimed herself with the descent of
the Holy Spirit on the apostles. Today I entrust to you
particularly the Church which has existed for many
centuries in this country and which represents a large
community of believers among peoples who speak the
same language. I commend to you, Mother, the whole
history of this Church and its tasks in the world of today:
its numerous initiatives and its tireless service for all the
inhabitants of the country, as well as for so many communities and Churches in the world, to which the
Christians of Germany send aid so willingly and generously.

Mary, you who are blessed, since you believed, I entrust
to you what seems to be the most important thing in the
service of the Church in this country: its powerful witness
of faith before the new generation of men and women of
this people, in the light of growing materialism and religious
indifference. May this witness always speak with the clear
words of the Gospel and thus find access to hearts,
particularly to those of the young generation. May it attract
the young and make them eager for a life according to the
image of the "new man" and for the various services in
the vineyard of the Lord.

Mother of Christ, who before his passion prayed:
"Father . . . that they may all be one! " (Jn 17: 11, 21),
how closely connected is my way through German land,
precisely this year, with the deep and humble longing for

unity among Christians, who have been divided since the 16th century! Can anyone desire more deeply than you that Christ's prayer in the Upper Room should come true? And if we ourselves must recognize that we shared responsibility for the division, and today pray for a new unity in love and in truth, could we not hope that you, Mother of Christ, will pray together with us? Could we not hope that the fruit of this prayer will in due time be the gift of that "fellowship of the Holy Spirit" (2 Cor 13 : 14), which is essential "so that the world may believe" (Jn 17 : 21)?

To you, Mother, I entrust the future of the faith in this ancient Christian country; and mindful of the sufferings of the last terrible war, which inflicted such deep wounds especially on the peoples of Europe. I entrust the peace of the world to you. May there arise among these peoples a new order, based on full respect for the rights of every single nation and of every individual in his nation, a really moral order, in which the peoples will be able to live together as in a family through the due balance of justice and freedom.

I address this prayer to you, Queen of Peace and Mirror of Justice, I, John Paul II, Bishop of Rome and the Successor of St Peter, and I leave it at your shrine in Altötting in lasting memory.   Amen.

(Altötting, 18.11.80—OR, 22.12.80)

FOR THE CHURCH IN AFRICA

26. On this day of joy as we gather in your presence, O Mary,
Mother of Jesus and Mother of his Church, we are mindful
of the role you played in the evangelization of this land.
We are mindful of how—in the beginning—the missionaries
came with the power of Christ's Gospel and committed
the success of their work to you.

As Mother of Divine Grace you were with the
missionaries in all their efforts, and you were with Mother
Church—of whom you are the type, the model and the
supreme expression—in bringing Christ into Africa.

And as Mother of the Church you presided over all
the activities of evangelization and over the implantation
of the Gospel in the hearts of the faithful. You sustained
the missionaries in hope and you gave joy to every new
community that was born of the Church's evangelizing
activity.

You were there with your intercession and your prayers,
as the first grace of baptism developed, and as those who
had new life in Christ your Son came to a full appreciation
of their sacramental life and Christian calling.

And you are here today as the Christian family gathers
to celebrate the Gospel, to recall the mighty works of God,
and to commit itself to the continued evangelization of this
land and continent "so that the word of the Lord may
speed on and triumph" (2 Thess 3 : 11).

We ask you, Mary, to help us to fulfil this mission which
your Son has given to his Church and which, in this
generation, falls to us. Mindful of your role as Help of
Christians, we entrust ourselves to you in the work of
carrying the Gospel ever deeper into the hearts and lives
of all the people. We entrust to you our missionary mandate
and commit our cause totally to your prayers.

And as Pastor of the universal Church, and Vicar of
your Son, I, John Paul II, through you, O Mary, entrust
the whole Church of Ghana and in all Africa to Christ
our Lord. Through you I present to Christ the Saviour

the destiny of Africa, praying that his love and justice will touch the heart of every man, woman and child of this continent.

Mary, I entrust all this to Christ through you, and I entrust all this to you for Christ your Son. I do it at a moment when I am closely united with my brother-bishops in celebrating the Gospel as "the power of salvation to all who believe" (Rom 1 : 16). I do it now, at this special moment when my brothers are so close to me in the exercise of our common responsibility for the Church in Africa. Accept, O Mary, this offering from all of us, and from all God's people, and present it to your Son. Present to him a Church "holy and without blemish" (Eph 5 : 27). Be mindful, O Mother, of all who make up the Church in Africa. Assist the bishops and their priests to be ever faithful to the word of God. Help to sanctify the religious and the seminarians. Intercede so that the love of your Son will penetrate in to all families, so that it will console all those in pain and suffering, all those in need and want. Look kindly upon the catechists and all who fulfil a special role in evangelization and Catholic education for the glory of your Son. Accept this our loving consecration and confirm us in the Gospel of your Son.

As we express our deepest gratitude to you for a century of your Maternal care, we are strong in the conviction that the Holy Spirit is still overshadowing you, so that in Africa you may bring forth Christ in every generation.

To Jesus Christ your Son, with the Father, in the unity of the Holy Spirit be praise and thanksgiving for ever and ever.   Amen.

(At the end of Mass in Accra, Ghana, 2.5.80—OR, 2.6.80)

FOR THE PEOPLES OF ASIA

27. On the threshold of my pastoral visit to the Far East I
commend to you and entrust to you with absolute confidence,
as to the Mother of our Redeemer, all the nations and
peoples of Asia and the surrounding islands. I commend
to you and entrust to you the Church, particularly in those
places where she is most in difficulty, where her mission
is not properly understood, not her irrepressible wish to
serve individuals and peoples. I commend to you today, on
the threshold of this pilgrimage, the hospitable Philippines
and the Church which, being rooted particularly strongly
here also feels particularly strongly its missionary
responsibility. May it not lack the strength needed for the
work of evangelization. May it persevere, like that faithful
servant who constantly awaits the coming of the Lord,
in the service of its own people and in openness to all others.

(At Shrine of Our Lady of Perpetual Help,
Baclaran, Philippines,
17.2.1981—OR, 23.2.1981)

FOR THE PEOPLE AND THE CHURCH OF BRAZIL

28. Our Lady Aparecida!

At this solemn and exceptional moment, I wish to open before you, O Mother, the heart of this people, in whose midst you have wished to dwell in such a special way —as in the midst of other nations and peoples—as in the midst of the nation whose son I am. I wish to lay open before you the heart of the Church and the heart of the world to which this Church was sent by your Son. I wish to open to you my heart also.

Our Lady Aparecida! The woman revealed by God to crush the serpent's head (cf. Gen 3 : 15) in your Immaculate Conception! Chosen from all eternity to be the Mother of the Eternal Word, who, at the annunciation of the angel, was conceived in your virginal womb as the Son of man and a real man!

United more closely to the mystery of the redemption of man and of the world, at the foot of the cross on Calvary!

Given on Calvary as Mother to all men in the person of John, the apostle and evangelist!

Given as Mother to the whole Church, from the community that was preparing for the coming of the Holy Spirit to the community of all those who are pilgrims on earth, in the course of the history of people and nations, of countries and continents, of eras and generations! . . .

Mary! I greet you and I say to you Ave! in this shrine where the Church of Brazil loves you, venerates you and invokes you as Aparecida, as revealed and given to her in a particular way. As her mother and patroness! As mediatrix and advocate with the Son whose Mother you are! As the model of all souls that possess true wisdom and, at the same time, the simplicity of the child, and that deep trust that overcomes all weakness and all suffering!

I wish to entrust to you particularly this people and this Church, this whole great and hospitable Brazil, all your sons and daughters, with all their problems and their worries, their activities and their joys. I wish to do so as the Successor of Peter and Pastor of the universal Church, entering into this heritage of veneration and love, dedication and trust, which for centuries has been part of the Church of Brazil and of all those who form it, without considering differences of origin, race, and social position, and wherever they live in this immense country. At this moment they have all been looking to Fortaleza and asking themselves: "Where are you going?"

O Mother! Let the Church be for this Brazilian people a sacrament of salvation and a sign of the unity of all men, adopted brothers and sisters of your Son and children of the heavenly Father!

O Mother! Let this Church, following the example of Christ by serving man constantly, defend everyone, especially the poor and the needy, those living on the fringes of society and in want. Let the Church of Brazil always be at the service of justice among men and at the same time contribute to the common good of all and to social peace.

O Mother! Open the hearts of men and let everyone understand that only in the spirit of the Gospel and observing the commandment of love and the beatitudes of the Sermon on the Mount will it be possible to construct a more human world, in which the dignity of all men will really be given new value.

O Mother! Let the Church, which in this land of Brazil has carried out a great work of evangelization in the past and whose history is rich in experience, accomplish her tasks today with new zeal, with new love of the mission received from Christ. For this purpose grant her numerous priestly and religious vocations, so that the whole people of God may benefit from the ministry of the stewards of the Eucharist and of the witnesses to the Gospel.

O Mother! Accept in your heart all Brazilian families! Accept all adults and old people, the young and children! Accept the sick and all those who live in solitude! Accept workers in the fields and factories, intellectuals in schools and universities, all those who are working in any institution. Protect them all!

Do not cease, O Virgin Aparecida, to demonstrate with your own presence in this land that love is stronger than death, more powerful than sin! Do not cease to show us God, who so loved the world that he gave it his only Son, that none of us should perish but have eternal life! (cf. Jn 3 : 16).   Amen.

(At the Dedication of the
National Basilica of Aparecida,
4.7.80—OR, 21.7.80)

29. Lady Aparecida, a son of yours
who belongs to you unreservedly
—totus tuus—
called by the mysterious plan of Providence to be
the Vicar of your Son on earth,
wishes to address you at this moment.
He recalls with emotion,
because of the brown colour of this image of yours,
another image of yours,
the Black Virgin of Jasna Gora!
Mother of God and our Mother,
protect the Church, the Pope, the bishops, the priests
and all the faithful people;
welcome under your protecting mantle
men and women religious, families, children, young
people and their educators!
Health of the sick and Consoler of the afflicted,
comfort those who are suffering in body and soul;
be the light of those who are seeking Christ,
the Redeemer of man;
show all men that you are the Mother of our confidence.
Queen of Peace and Mirror of Justice,
obtain peace for the world,
ensure that Brazil may have lasting peace,
that men will always live together as brothers,
as sons of God!
Our Lady Aparecida,
bless this shrine of yours and those who work in it,
bless this people praying and singing here,
bless all your sons,
bless Brazil.   Amen.

(From the homily at the Mass in the
Basilica of Aparecida,
4.7.80—OR, 21.7.80)

FOR CATHOLICS IN THE CONGO

30. And now, Lord, I beseech you for my brothers and sisters, the Catholics of the Congo. I entrust them to you, since you have permitted me to visit them in their country. I commend to you their faith, young but how full of vitality, that it may grow, that it may be pure and beautiful, and communicative, that it may continue to express itself and to be freely proclaimed, for eternal life is that they know the only true God and Jesus Christ, whom he sent (cf. Jn 17: 13). I entrust them also to your holy Mother, the Blessed Virgin Mary, Mother of the Church and our Mother. May she take them under her motherly protection and watch over them in their difficulties! May she teach them to stand at the foot of your cross and to gather around her while waiting for your coming, at the end of time!

With them, I pray to you for their unity, which has its source in you, and without which their testimony would be weakened: unity of the episcopal body, unity in the clergy and in the dioceses, capacity of collaborating beyond all ethnical or social differences, unity also with Peter's See and the Church as a whole. You cannot close your ears to this prayer, you who gave yourself up to gather the children of God.

Listen further to the intention we address to you on this day for the sanctification of priests, men and women religious, and all those who, in the various formation centres, are preparing to consecrate their lives to you. Answering your call, may they be able to renounce for you the things of this world, and all pursuit of material and human glory, and be available for the urgent needs of the Church in any mission that will be entrusted to them (cf. Ad Gentes, 20). Rejoicing in their total gift, rejoicing in their celibacy, may they experience more and more deeply, they for whom the Eucharist marks the peak point of all their days, what it means to offer one's life as a sacrifice for the salvation of men.

In your goodness, I know that you will remember

particularly the sacrifice for the salvation of men.

In your goodness, I know that you will remember particularly the sacrifice of missionaries, who, out of love for you, left their country of origin, their families, everything they had, to come and live in the midst of their Congolese brothers, to love this people, become theirs and to serve it. Reward such generosity, Lord! Let it be recognized, let it bring forth other vocations, let it awaken a real missionary spirit in everyone.

Surround with your benevolence also and particularly your humble servants, the bishops, to whom you have entrusted these local Churches. I am beside them, this morning, to strengthen them in your name. They are there, the three pastors of the Congo, and most of their confrères in the neighbouring Episcopal Conferences with whom they usually meet under the presidency, today, of Archbishop N'Dayen of Bangui. There are even some bishops from other nearby countries. They have brought their pastoral concerns and all the intentions with which their communities have charged them. Yes, as you asked of Peter and his successors, I wish to bring them the calm strength and the certainty of your help in their daily toil, which is so meritorious. And I wish to assure those who have not been able to join us of my brotherly and spiritual closeness, to take a part of their burden on my shoulders, while some of them are suffering so cruelly from the sufferings of their people. Dear confrères of Chad, I am thinking of you in the first place, and of the flock entrusted to you. May God help you to dress wounds and to cure hearts! May he give you peace!

(In the Cathedral of Brazzaville
in the Congo,
5.5.80—OR, 26.5.80)

FOR IRELAND

31. *Mother*, in this shrine you gather the people of God of
all Ireland and constantly point out to them Christ in the
Eucharist and in the Church. At this solemn moment
we listen with particular attention to your words: "Do
whatever my Son tells you". And *we wish* to respond
to your words with all our heart. We wish to do what your
Son tells us, for he has the words of eternal life. We wish
to carry out and fulfil all that comes from him, all that is
contained in the Good News, as our forefathers did for
many centuries. Their fidelity to Christ and to his Church,
and their heroic attachment to the Apostolic See, have in
a way stamped on all of us an indelible mark that we all
share. Their fidelity has, over the centuries, borne fruit
in Christian heroism and in a virtuous tradition of living
in accordance with God's law, especially in accordance with
the holiest commandment of the Gospel—the commandment
of love. We have received this splendid heritage from their
hands at the beginning of a new age, as we approach the
close of the second millennium since the Son of God was
born of you, our *alma mater,* and we intend to *carry this
heritage into the future* with the same fidelity with which
our forefathers bore witness to it.

Today, therefore, on the occasion of the first visit of
a Pope to Ireland, we entrust and consecrate to you, Mother
of Christ and Mother of the Church, our hearts, our
consciences, and our works, in order that they may be in
keeping with the faith we profess. We entrust and consecrate
to you each and every one of those who make up both
the community of the Irish people and the community
of the people of God living in this land.

We entrust and consecrate to you the bishops of
Ireland, the religious men and women, the contemplative
monks and sisters, the seminarians, the novices. We entrust
and consecrate to you the mothers and fathers, the youth,
the children. We entrust and consecrate to you the
teachers, the catechists, the students, the writers, the poets,

the actors, the artists, the workers and their leaders, the employers and managers, the professional people; those engaged in political and public life; those who form public opinion. We entrust and consecrate to you the married and those preparing for marriage; those called to serve you and their fellow-men in single life; the sick, the aged, the mentally ill, the handicapped and all who nurse and care for them. We entrust and consecrate to you the prisoners and all who feel rejected; the exiled, the homesick and the lonely.

We entrust to your motherly care the land of Ireland, where you have been and are so much loved. Help this land to stay true to you and your Son always. May prosperity never cause Irish men and women to forget God or abandon their faith. Keep them faithful in prosperity to the faith they would not surrender in poverty and persecution. Save them from greed, from envy, from seeking selfish or sectional interest. Help them to work together with a sense of Christian purpose and a common Christian goal, to build a just and peaceful and loving society where the poor are never neglected and the rights of all, especially the weak, are respected. Queen of Ireland, Mary, Mother of the heavenly and earthly Church, Máthair Dé, keep Ireland true to her spiritual tradition and her Christian heritage. Help her to respond to her historic mission of bringing the light of Christ to the nations, and so making the glory of God be the honour of Ireland.

Mother, can we keep silent about what we find most painful, what leaves us many a time so helpless? In a very special way we entrust to you this great wound now afflicting our people, hoping that your hands will be able to cure and heal it. Great is our concern for those young souls who are caught up in bloody acts of vengeance and hatred. Mother, do not abandon these youthful hearts. Mother, be with them in their most dreadful hours, when we can neither counsel nor assist them. Mother, protect all of us and especially the youth of Ireland from being overcome by hostility and hatred. Teach us to distinguish clearly what proceeds from love for our country from what bears the mark of destruction and the brand of Cain. Teach us that evil means can never lead to a good end;

that all human life is sacred; that murder is murder no matter what the motive or end. Save others, those who view these terrible events, from another danger: that of living a life robbed of Christian ideals or in conflict with the principles of morality.

May our ears constantly hear with the proper clarity your motherly voice: "Do whatever my Son tells you". Enable us to *persevere with Christ*. Enable us, Mother of the Church, to *build up his Mystical Body* by living with the life that he alone can grant us from his fullness, which is both divine and human.

(At the Shrine of Our Lady of Knock,
30.9.79—OR, 8.10.79)

FOR ITALY AND EUROPE

32. Today we are praying in this place. We are praying for Italy and for Europe in the Saint's birthplace. We are praying for individuals and families, for the peoples and for the Church. We are praying for peace in Europe and throughout the world. We are praying for human freedom, in keeping with the dignity of man's ideas and works. We are praying for social justice and genuine love, without which human life is to some extent stifled. We are praying for an end to the fearsome menace to mankind brought by the modern means of destruction, and an end to the menace hidden in the hearts of people who are ready to kill and destroy.

On this day of reflection and prayer promoted by the Italian Episcopal Conference, we are asking the Lord to touch the hearts and stay the hands of all those involved in the dark plots and hatred and crime. We are praying that all may feel it their duty to work together in order to isolate these senseless atrocities and to bear witness, in their own lives, to the priceless values of peace, brotherhood and mutual love. As I had occasion to say in Ireland, so now I repeat to all those who may be entangled in the sad phenomenon of terrorism, "that violence is evil, that violence is unacceptable as a solution to problems, that violence is unworthy of man. Violence is a lie for it goes against the truth of our faith, the truth of our humanity. Violence destroys what it claims to defend: the dignity, the life, the freedom of human beings" (Homily at Drogheda, 29 September 1979).

Through the intercession of St Benedict, the peacemaker and bringer of concord in centuries that knew the division caused by hatred and barbarity, may the forces of evil fall, those forces that have been unleashed in the world and in human hearts, so that the face of the earth may be renewed: the face of this place, and of this continent of which he is the patron.

Let us also pray for the Church, which, in the midst

of earthly trials, is seeking her unity in Christ. This is her never ceasing conversion. Especially at the present time of penance and conversion. May the Church be converted to Christ, to her Lord and Redeemer, Teacher and Spouse!

(Norcia, the birthplace of St Benedict,
23.3.80—OR, 31.3.80)

E

FOR THE CHURCH OF JAPAN

33. Having been given the opportunity to visit this house, marked as it is by the memory of Blessed Maximilian Kolbe, I wish to draw, in a certain sense, from the spirit of that apostolic zeal which once led him to Japan, and to utter the words which that son of St Francis, the living flame of love, seems to speak to us still.

These words are addressed to you, the Immaculate Virgin. It was you that Father Maximilian preached—you, the one eternally chosen to be the Mother of the Son of God; you, the one whom the stain of original sin never touched, because of that holy motherhood; you, the one who became his Mother and the Mother of our hope.

Permit me, John Paul II, Bishop of Rome and the Successor of St Peter, and at the same time a son of the same nation as Blessed Maximilian Kolbe—permit me, Immaculate One, to entrust to you the Church of your Son, the Church that for more than four hundred years has been carrying out her mission in Japan. This is that ancient Church of the great martyrs and inflexible confessors. And it is the Church of the present day, making her way once more through the service of the bishops, through the work of the priests, religious brothers and sisters, whether Japanese or missionary, and through the witness of the lay Christians that live in their families and in the various spheres of society, shaping its culture and civilization every day, and working for the common good.

This Church is truly that "little flock" of the Gospel, just like the first disciples and confessors—the little flock to whom Christ said: "Fear not . . . for it is your Father's good pleasure to give you the kingdom" (Lk 12 : 32).

O Immaculate Mother of the Church, through your humble intercession with your Son, grant that this "little flock" may become day by day a more eloquent sign of the kingdom of God in Japan! Grant that, through it, that kingdom may shine ever more brightly in people's lives and spread to others through the grace of faith and through holy baptism. May it grow ever stronger through the exemplary Christian lives of the sons and daughters of the Church in Japan. May it grow strong in expectation of the coming of the Lord, when the history of the world will be accomplished in God alone.

This I entrust to you, O Immaculate One, and this I implore of Christ through the intercession of all the holy and blessed Japanese martyrs, and of Blessed Maximilian Kolbe, the apostle who loved this land so much.   Amen.

(At the Church of the Immaculate
Conception, Nagasaki,
26.2.81—OR, 16.3.81)

FOR MEXICO AND LATIN AMERICA

34. Let me, John Paul II, Bishop of Rome and Pope, together with my brothers in the episcopate representing the Church in Mexico and in the whole of Latin America, at this solemn moment entrust and offer to you, the handmaid of the Lord, the whole heritage of the Gospel, the cross and the resurrection, of which we are all witnesses, apostles, teachers and bishops.

O Mother, help us to be faithful stewards of the great mysteries of God. Help us to teach the truth proclaimed by your Son and to spread love, which is the chief commandment and the first fruit of the Holy Spirit. Help us to strengthen our brethren in faith, help us to awaken hope in eternal life. Help us to guard the great treasures stored in the souls of the people of God entrusted to us.

We offer you the whole of this people of God. We offer you the Church in Mexico and in the whole continent. We offer it to you as your own. You have entered so deeply into the hearts of the faithful through that sign of your presence constituted by your image in the shrine of Guadalupe. Be at home in these hearts, for the future also. Be at home in our families, our parishes, missions, dioceses, and in all the peoples.

Do this through the holy Church, for she, in imitation of you, Mother, wishes in her turn to be a good mother and to care for souls in all their needs by proclaiming the Gospel, administering the sacraments, safeguarding family life with the sacrament of matrimony, gathering all into the eucharistic community by means of the Holy Sacrament of the Altar, and by being lovingly with them from the cradle until they enter eternity.

O Mother, awaken in the younger generation a readiness for the exclusive service of God. Implore for us abundant local vocations to the priesthood and the consecrated life.

O Mother, strengthen the faith of our brothers and sisters in the laity, so that in every field of social, professional, cultural and political life they may act in accordance with the truth and the law brought by your Son to mankind, in order to lead everyone to eternal salvation and, at the same time, to make life on earth more human, more worthy of man.

The Church is carrying out her task among the American nations; the Church in Mexico wishes to serve this sublime cause with all her strength and with a renewed missionary spirit. Mother, enable us to serve the Church in truth and justice. Make us follow this way ourselves and lead others, without ever straying along twisted paths and dragging others with us.

We offer and entrust to you everyone and everything for which we have pastoral responsibility, confident that you will be with us and will help us to carry out what your Son has told us to do (cf. Jn 2 : 5). We bring you this unlimited trust. With trust I, John Paul II, with all my brothers in the episcopate of Mexico and Latin America, wish to bind you still more strongly to the life of our nations. We wish to place in your hands the whole of our future, the future of evangelization in Latin America.

Queen of the Apostles, accept our readiness to serve unreservedly the cause of your Son, the cause of the Gospel, and the cause of peace based on justice and love between individuals and peoples.

Queen of Peace, save the nations and peoples of the whole continent—they have so much trust in you—from wars, hatred and subversion.

Make everybody, whether they are rulers or subjects, learn to live in peace, educate themselves for peace, and do what is demanded by justice and respect for the rights of every person, so that peace may be firmly established.

Accept our trustful offering, O handmaid of the Lord. May your maternal presence in the mystery of Christ and of the Church become a source of joy and freedom for each and every one, a source of that freedom through which "Christ has set us free" (Gal 5 : 1), and in the end a source of that peace that the world cannot give but which is only given by him, by Christ (cf. Jn 14 : 27).

Finally, O Mother, recalling and confirming the gesture of my predecessors Benedict XIV and Pius X, who proclaimed you Patroness of Mexico and of the whole of

Latin America, I present to you a diadem in the name of
all your Mexican and Latin American children, that you may
keep them under your protection, preserve their harmony
in faith and their fidelity to Christ, your Son.   Amen.

(In the Basilica of Our Lady
of Guadalupe,
27.1.79—OR, 5.2.79)

FOR POLAND

35. And now, dear countrymen, regarding the news which has come from Poland, I wish to read again before you present here, or rather to recite two prayers which the Polish Church uses: the first on the solemnity of Mary, Queen of Poland, on 3 May, and the second on the solemnity of Our Lady of Czestochowa on 26 August.

"O God, who hast given the Polish nation, in the most holy Virgin Mary, a wonderful help and shield, graciously grant that through the intercession of our Mother and Queen, the Church may always enjoy freedom, and the country, peace and security."

"Assist, O Lord, the people which you strengthen with your body and blood, and through the intercession of your most holy Mother, deliver them from all evil and every danger, and surround with your protection all their good works."

These prayers by themselves say how much we here in Rome are united with our fellow Poles and with the Church in particular, whose problems are close to the heart, and for which we ask the Lord's aid.

(General Audience,
20.8.80—OR, 25.8.80)

36. Our Lady of the Bright Mountain, Mother of the Church! *Once more I consecrate myself to you "in your maternal slavery of love": Totus tuus!* —I am all yours! I consecrate to you the whole Church—everywhere and to the ends of the earth! I consecrate to you humanity; I consecrate to you all men and women, my brothers and sisters. All the peoples and the nations. I consecrate to you Europe and all the continents. I consecrate to you Rome and Poland, united through your servant, by a fresh bond of love.

71

Mother, accept us!
Mother, do not abandon us!
Mother, be our guide!

(Monastery of Jasna Gora,
6.6.79—OR, 6.7.79)

FOR THE CHURCH IN ZAIRE

37. At the moment when the Church, in this country of Zaïre, thanks God in the Holy Trinity for the waters of holy baptism that gave salvation to so many of its sons and daughters, permit me, O Mother of Christ and Mother of the Church, permit me, Pope John Paul II, who has the privilege of taking part in this jubilee, *to recall and at the same time renew this missionary consecration* which took place in this land at the beginning of its evangelization.

To consecrate itself to Christ through you!

To consecrate itself to you for Christ!

Permit me also, O Mother of Divine Grace, while expressing my thanks for all the light that the Church has received and for all the fruit she has yielded in this country of Zaïre in the course of this century, to entrust this Church to you again, to place it in your hands again for the years and the centuries to come, to the end of time!

And at the same time, I entrust to you also the whole nation, which is living its own independent life today. I do so *in the same spirit of faith* and with the same *trust* as the first missionaries, and I do so at the same time *with all the greater joy* since the act of consecration and abandonment that I make now is made with me at the same time by all the *pastors* of this Church and also by the whole *people of God*: this people of God that wishes to assume and continue with its pastors, in love and apostolic courage, the work of the construction of the Body of Christ and the approach of the Kingdom of God on this earth.

Accept, O Mother, this act of trust of ours, *open hearts,* and *give strength to souls* to listen to the word of life and to do what your Son constantly orders and urges on us.

May grace and peace, justice and love be the lot of this people; giving thanks for the centenary of its faith and its baptism, may it look confidently towards its temporal and eternal future!   Amen!

(In the Cathedral of Kinshasa, Zaïre,
2.5.80—OR, 12.5.80)

73

FOR THE PAST MISSIONARIES TO ZAIRE

38. Kneeling in this cemetery at the tomb of the missionaries
come from afar, we pray to you, Lord.

Blessed be you, Lord, for the testimony of your
missionaries! It was you who inspired their apostolic hearts
to leave for ever their land, their family, their native
country, to come to this country, unknown to them until
then, and to propose the Gospel to those whom they
already considered brothers.

Blessed be you, Lord, for having supported their faith
and their hope, at sowing time; and throughout their
apostolic labour; for having given them resistance and
patience in toil, difficulties, sorrows and sufferings of
every kind.

Blessed be you, Lord, for having strengthened their
attachment and trust to the sons of this people, to the
extent of considering them, very soon, capable of the life
of the baptized and opening to them the way to religious
life, to priestly preparation, with the tenacious will of
founding, with them and for them, a local Church, the
fruits of which we are gathering.

Blessed be you, Lord, for all the graces that have come
through their word, through their hands, through their
example.

They dedicated their lives to the end for the mission,
and they left their mortal remains to this land; some after
a life shortened by work, some even after a life risked and
offered as martyrs for the faith. The grain of wheat had to
fall into the earth and die in order to yield much fruit.

Lord, bring it about that the Church watered by their
sweat and their blood may reach its full maturity. Thanks
to them, others can harvest today in joy what they sowed
in tears. May large numbers come forth among the sons
and daughters of this country, to take over from them, in
order that your name may be glorified in this African land.

Let us take care not to forget these pioneers of the
Gospel, in the memory of the heart and of prayer. We hope

that you have welcomed them into your paradise, forgiving
the weaknesses that may have marked their lives like those
of all human beings. Give them the reward of good and
faithful servants. May they enter the joy of their Master.
Give them eternal rest and may your light shine upon
them for ever.   Amen.

(At the Cemetery of Makiso,
Kisangani, Zaïre,
6.5.80—OR, 26.5.80)

AT THE TOMB OF ST ALBERT THE GREAT

39. God, thou art wondrous in thy saints!

Appointed by you to the highest office of the Church of Jesus Christ, I kneel today as a pilgrim at the tomb of St Albert, to glorify you with all the faithful on this day commemorating the 700th anniversary of his death, and to thank you for his life and his works, through which you gave him to your Church as a teacher of the faith and an example of Christian life.

God, our creator, cause and light of the human spirit, you gave St Albert a profound knowledge of faith in true imitation of our Lord and Master Jesus Christ. The world itself became for him the revelation of your omnipotence and goodness.

Through his contact with your creation he learned to recognize and love you more profoundly. At the same time he researched through the works of human wisdom, including the writings of non-Christian philosophers, and paved the way for their encounter with your Gospel.

Through the gift of discrimination you made him uniquely able to avoid error, to establish truth more deeply and make it known among men. In doing so you made him a teacher of the Church and of all mankind.

With the intercession of St Albert we pray together to you for your mercy:

—Send to your Church teachers of truth in our time as well, who will be capable of interpreting and preaching your Gospel to the people of the world through their words and saintly living. Hear us, O Lord.

—Open the hearts of men through the grace of a living faith so that they may recognize God's presence in his creation and their own lives and come to correspond more and more perfectly with his holy will.

—Accompany and illuminate the work of scientists and scholars with your Holy Spirit. Preserve them from pride and self-conceit and give them a sense of responsibility in their dealings with the gifts of your creation.

—Give those responsible in State and society insight and responsibility so that they may use the achievements of science and technology for peace and progress among the peoples of the world and not for their harm or destruction.

—Help us all to recognise the truth amidst the many dangers and errors of our time and to serve you devoutly in a life strenthened by faith.

—With the intercession of St Albert bless all the citizens of this country, give the German people peace and unity and let it always be aware of its responsibility in the community of nations.

—Accompany my pastoral visit in the Federal Republic of Germany with your special blessings and assistance, strengthen all believers in their love of Christ and his Church so that through the testimony of their Christian living your name may be glorified in truth and justice in the world today.

Pray for us, St Albert, that we may be made worthy of the promises of Christ.

Let us pray: God, our refuge and strength, you gave the saintly bishop and teacher of the Church, Albert, the power to associate human knowledge with eternal wisdom. With his intercession, strengthen and protect our faith in the intellectual confusion of our days. Give us the openness of his intellect so that the progress of science may also help us to know you more profoundly and come closer to you. Let us grow in the knowledge of the truth which you yourself are so that we may one day see you face to face in the presence of all the saints. For this we pray through Christ our Lord.   Amen.

(Church of St Andrew, Cologne,
15.11.80—OR, 24.11.80)

TO SAINTS CYRIL AND METHODIUS

40. O Saints Cyril and Methodius, who brought the faith with admirable dedication to peoples thirsty for the truth and the light, let the whole Church always proclaim the crucified and the Risen Christ, the Redeemer of man!

O Saints Cyril and Methodius, who, in your hard and difficult missionary apostolate always remained deeply bound to the Church of Constantinople and to the Roman See of Peter, bring it about that the two sister Churches, the Catholic Church and the Orthodox, having overcome the elements of division in charity and truth, may soon reach the full union desired!

O Saints Cyril and Methodius, who with the sincere spirit of brotherhood, approached different peoples to bring to all the message of universal love preached by Christ, bring it about that the peoples of the European continent, aware of their common Christian heritage, may live in mutual respect for just rights and in solidarity, and be peacemakers among all the nations of the world!

O Saints Cyril and Methodius, who, driven by love for Christ, abandoned everything to serve the Gospel, protect the Church of God: me, Peter's successor in the Roman See; the bishops, priests, men and women religious, men and women missionaries, fathers, mothers, young men, young women, the poor, the sick, and the suffering; may each of us, in the place in which Divine Providence has placed us, be a worthy "labourer" of the Lord's harvest! Amen!

(Homily in the Church of
San Clemente, Rome,
14.2.81—OR, 16.3.81)

AT THE TOMB OF ST FRANCIS OF ASSISI

41. Help us, St Francis of Assisi, to bring Christ closer to the
Church and to the world of today. You who bore in your
heart the vicissitudes of your contemporaries, help us, with
our heart close to the Redeemer's heart, to embrace the lives
of the people of our time. The difficult social, economic
and political problems, the problems of culture and
contemporary civilization, all the sufferings of the people
today, their doubts, their denials, their disorders, their
tensions, their complexes, their worries . . . Help us to
express all this in the simple and faithful language of the
Gospel. Help us to solve everything on an evangelical level,
in order that Christ himself may be "the Way, the Truth
and the Life" for the people of our time.

This is asked of you, holy son of the Church, son of the
Italian land, by Pope John Paul II, son of Poland. And
he hopes that you will not refuse him it, that you will help
him. You have always been kind and you have always
hastened to bring help to all those who appealed to you.

(In the Basilica of St Francis of Assisi,
5.11.78—OR, 16.11.78)

ON THE FEAST OF ST JOSEPH

42. Let us raise together our prayer to God, through the intercession of St Joseph, the head of the Holy Family of Nazareth and Patron Saint of the universal Church.

Let us pray together and say: Lord hear us!

1. For all the pastors and ministers of the Church, that they may serve the people of God with active and generous dedication, as St Joseph served the Lord Jesus and his Virgin Mother in a worthy way, Lord hear us!

2. For the public authorities, that in the service of the common good they may direct economic and social life with justice and uprightness, in respect for the rights and dignity of all, Lord hear us!

3. That God may deign to unite with the passion of his Son the toil and suffering of the workers, the anguish of the unemployed, the grief of the oppressed, and that he may give help and comfort to everyone, Lord hear us!

4. For all our families and for all their members: parents, children, the old, relatives, that, in respect for the life and personality of each one, they may all collaborate in the growth of faith and charity, to be real witnesses of the Gospel, Lord hear us!

O Lord, bestow on your faithful the Spirit of truth and peace, that they may know you with all their soul, and generously carrying out what pleases you, may always enjoy your benefits.

Through Christ our Lord.
Amen.

(General Audience, Rome,
19.3.80—OR, 24.3.80)

ON THE FEAST OF SAINTS
PETER AND PAUL

43. Blessed are you, Paul of Tarsus, the apostle of the Gentiles,
the converted persecutor, the admirable lover and witness
of the crucified and Risen Christ! Blessed are you, the
apostle of Rome, rooted together with Peter in the very
beginning of the Church in this capital. Blessed are you,
steward of the mysteries of God—you, for whom "to live
is Christ" (Phil 1 : 21); you, who desire so much and so
exclusively to be called the minister of Christ—and who
desire to be only that—so that your and our Master speaks
in you. She, whom the Father chose to be the Mother of
his eternal Son, also speaks in the same way. She was the
first to say of herself: "Behold, I am the handmaid of
the Lord"!

We bless you Paul and Peter, on the day of your joint
feast, and we thank God because before this city—and
before the world—you became such great witnesses to the
truth, according to which "the Word became flesh and
dwelt among us" (Jn 1 : 14).

I address you, Holy Apostles of the Church and of
Rome, on the eve of the journey which I have the privilege
of undertaking tomorrow, to answer the call that has come
from great Brazil. May I, following you, Peter, proclaim
everywhere Christ, who is the Son of the Living God and
who, alone has "the words of eternal life" (Jn 6 : 68).

May I, following you, Paul, repeat: let no one think
of us differently from what we are, namely, "servants of
Christ and stewards of the mysteries of God" (1 Cor 4 : 1).

May Mary, the handmaid of the Lord, accompany
this pilgrimage and my whole pastoral service.

("Angelus", St Peter's Square,
29.6.80—OR, 7.7.80)

F

TO ST STANISLAUS, PATRON OF POLAND

44. St Stanislaus, our Patron, the protector of the whole
country, help us, teach us to be victorious, teach us to
attain victory from day to day. Patron of the moral order
in our country, show us how we must attain it, by carrying
out the work of indispensable renewal, which begins in man,
in every man, which embraces the whole of society and
all the dimensions of its life: spiritual, cultural, social and
economic, spiritual and cultural, spiritual and material.
Teach us this. Teach us and help us, you who are, together
with the Queen of Poland of Jasna Gora and with St
Adalbert, the Patron Saint of our country. Help us to
attain this victory in our generation.   Amen.

(Vatican Grotto, Feast of St Stanislaus,
8.5.81—OR, 18.5.81)

TO THE MOST RECENT 'BEATI'

45. As we bow reverently before them, we entrust ourselves
to their powerful intercession:

O Blessed Alain de Solminihac,
O Blessed Luigi Scrosoppi,
O Blessed Riccardo Pampuri,
O Blessed Claudine Thevenet,
O Blessed Maria Repetto,

pray to the Holy Trinity for your earthly countries, that
they may live in serene concord! Pray for your Religious
Families, that they may give to modern society a joyful
witness of their donation to God! Pray for the Church,
a pilgrim on earth, that she may always be a sign and
instrument of deep union with God and of the unity of
the whole of mankind!

Pray for all the peoples in the world, that they may
realize justice and peace in their relations!

O new "Beati" men and women, pray for us!   Amen.

(Rome, 4.10.81—OR, 12.10.81)

FOR THE FAMILY

46. Lord God, from you every family in heaven and on earth takes its name. Father, you are Love and Life.

Through your Son, Jesus Christ, born of woman, and through the Holy Spirit, the fountain of divine charity, grant that every family on earth may become for each successive generation a true shrine of life and love.

Grant that your grace may guide the thoughts and actions of husbands and wives for the good of their families and of all the families in the world.

Grant that the young may find in the family solid support for their human diginity and for their growth in truth and love.

Grant that love, strengthened by the grace of the sacrament of marriage, may prove mightier than all the weaknesses and trials through which our families sometimes pass.

Through the intercession of the Holy Family of Nazareth, grant that the Church may fruitfully carry out her worldwide mission in the family and through the family.

We ask this of you, who are Life, Truth, and Love with the Son and the Holy Spirit.   Amen.

(Prayer for the 1980 Synod of Bishops
—OR, 25.8.80)

FOR PEACE

47. "Deliver us from evil"! Reciting these words of Christ's prayer, it is very difficult to give them a different content from the one that opposes peace, that destroys it, that threatens it. Let us pray therefore: Deliver us from war, from hatred, from the destruction of human lives! Do not allow us to kill! Do not allow the use of those means which are in the service of death and destruction and whose power, range of action, and precision go beyond the limits known hitherto.

Do not allow them to be used ever! "Deliver us from evil!" Defend us from war! From any war, Father, who are in heaven. Father of life and giver of peace, the Pope, the son of a nation which, during its history, and particularly in our century, has been among those most sorely tried in the horror, the cruelty, and the cataclysm of war, supplicates you. He supplicates you for all the peoples in the world, for all countries and for all continents. He supplicates you in the name of Christ, the Prince of Peace.

Mother, you know what it means to clasp in your arms the dead body of your Son, of him to whom you gave birth. Spare all mothers on this earth the death of their sons, the torments, the slavery, the destruction of war, the persecutions, the concentration camps, the prisons! Keep for them the joy of birth, of sustenance, of the development of man and of his life. In the name of this life, in the name of the birth of the Lord, implore peace for us, and justice in the world!

Mother of Peace, in all the beauty and majesty of your motherhood, which the Church exalts and the world admires, we pray to you: Be with us at every moment! Let this New Year be a year of peace, in virtue of the birth and death of your Son!   Amen.

(Homily, St Peter's, Rome
1.1.79—OR, 8.1.79)

48. And to the Creator of nature and man, of truth and beauty I pray:

Hear my voice, for it is the voice of the victims of all wars and violence among individuals and nations.

Hear my voice, for it the voice of all children who suffer and will suffer when people put their faith in weapons and war.

Hear my voice when I beg you to instil into the hearts of all human beings the wisdom of peace, the strength of justice and the joy of fellowship.

Hear my voice, for I speak for the multitudes in every country and in every period of history who do not want war and are ready to walk the road of peace.

Hear my voice and grant insight and strength so that we may always respond to hatred with love, to injustice with total dedication to justice, to need with the sharing of self, to war with peace.

O God, hear my voice and grant unto the world your everlasting peace.

(Hiroshima, 25.2.81—OR, 9.3.81)

FOR CONSOLATION

49. The Blessed Virgin continues to be the loving consoler of
humanity in the many physical and moral sufferings that
afflict and torment it. She knows our sorrows and our griefs,
because she, too, suffered from Bethlehem to Calvary: "and
a sword will pierce through your own soul too" (Lk 2 : 35).
Mary is our spiritual Mother, and a mother always
understands her own children and consoles them in their
troubles.

She had, moreover, from Jesus on the cross that specific
mission to love us, and only and always to love us in order
to save us! Mary consoles us above all by pointing out
to us Christ crucified, and paradise.

O Blessed Virgin, be the one and perennial consolation
of the Church that you love and protect! Console your
bishops and your priests, missionaries, and religious, who
must illumine and save modern society, which is difficult
and sometimes hostile! Console Christian communities
giving them the gift of numerous, strong priestly and
religious vocations!

Console all those who are invested with authority and
civil and religious responsibilities, so that we may have as
our goal, always and only, the common good and man's
complete development, in spite of difficulties and defeats!

Console . . . the many families of migrants, the
unemployed, the suffering, those who bear in their body
and soul the wounds caused by dramatic situations of
emergency; the young, especially those who, for so many
tragic reasons, are confused and disheartened; all those who
feel in their hearts an ardent need of love, altruism, charity,
and dedication, who cultivate high ideals of spiritual and
social conquests!

O consoling Mother, console us all, and make everyone
understand that the secret of happiness lies in goodness,
and in always following faithfully your Son, Jesus.

(At the Consolata Basilica, Turin,
21.4.80—OR, 28.4.80)

FOR CHRISTIAN UNITY

50. *Spouse of the Holy Spirit and Seat of Wisdom,* help us in
the great endeavour that we are carrying out *to meet on a
more and more mature way our brothers in the faith,*
with whom so many things unite us, although there is
still something dividing us. Through all the means of
knowledge, of mutual respect, of love, shared collaboration
in various fields, may we be able to rediscover gradually the
divine plan for the unity into which we should enter and
bring everybody in, in order that the one fold of Christ
may recognize and live its unity on earth. *Mother of unity,*
teach us constantly the ways that lead to unity.

Allow us in the future to go out *to meet human beings
and all the peoples* that are seeking God and wishing to
serve him on the way *of different religions.* Help us all to
proclaim Christ and reveal "the power of God and the
Wisdom of God" (1 Cor 1 : 24) hidden in his cross. You
were the first to reveal him at Bethlehem, not only to the
simple faithful shepherds but also to the wise men from
distant lands.

Mother of Good Counsel, show us always how we are
to serve the individual and humanity in every nation, how
we are to lead them along the ways of salvation. How we are
to protect *justice and peace* in a world continually threatened
on various sides. How greatly I desire on the occasion of our
meeting today, to entrust to you all the *difficult problems*
of the societies, systems and states—problems that cannot
be solved with hatred, war and self-destruction but only by
peace, justice and respect for the rights of people and
nations.

(At Jasna Gora,
4.6.79—OR, 11.6.79)

51. And now, dear brothers and sisters, let us unite in prayer
and make ours the intentions set forth above, with the

following invocations, to which you are all invited to answer: "Listen to us, O Lord!"

—In the spirit of Christ, our Lord, let us pray for the Catholic Church, for the other Churches, for the whole of mankind.

All: Listen to us, O Lord!

—Let us pray for all those who suffer persecution for the sake of justice and for those who are striving for freedom and peace.

All: Listen to us, O Lord!

—Let us pray for those who exercise a ministry in the Church, for those who have special responsibilities in social life, and for all those who are in the service of the little and the weak.

All: Listen to us, O Lord!

—Let us ask God for ourselves for the courage to persevere in our commitment for the realization of the unity of all Christians.

All: Listen to us, O Lord!

Lord God we trust in you. Grant that we may act in a way that is pleasing to you. Grant that we may be faithful servants of your glory.   Amen.

(General Audience during the
Week of Prayer for Christian Unity,
17.1.79—OR, 22.1.79)

52. Certainly on the way to unity there still exist serious difficulties, both of theological and of a psychological nature. Precisely for this reason the week of prayer, while it raises to God the harmonious chorus of the voices of all Christians imploring unity, must renew and strengthen commitment, warm our hearts and fortify hope.

Let us, too, therefore, now raise our prayer, and say together: *"That they may all be one"*.

That, straightaway Christians may bear common witness to the service of his kingdom. Let us pray!

All: That they may all be one.

That all Christian communities may unite in the pursuit of full unity. Let us pray!

All: That they may all be one.

That the perfect unity of all Christians may be realized so that God may be glorified by all men in Christ the Lord. Let us pray!

All: That they may all be one.

That all peoples on earth may overcome conflicts and selfishness and find full reconciliation and peace in the kingdom of God. Let us pray!

All: That they may all be one.

Let us pray: Remember your Church, O Lord: preserve her from all evil: make her perfect in your love; sanctify her and gather her from the four winds into your kingdom, which you have prepared for her. For yours is the power and the glory for ever and ever (Didache 10, 5).

All: Amen.

(General Audience during the
Week of Prayer for Christian Unity,
23.1.80—OR, 28.1.80)

53. —Let us ask the Lord to strengthen in all Christians faith in Christ, the Saviour of the world.

Listen to us, O Lord.

—Let us ask the Lord to sustain and guide Christians with his gifts along the way to full unity.

Listen to us, O Lord.

—Let us ask the Lord for the gift of unity and peace for the world.

Listen to us, O Lord.

—Let us pray: We ask you, O Lord, for the gifts of your Spirit. Enable us to penetrate the depth of the whole truth, and grant that we may share with others the goods that you put at our disposal.

Teach us to overcome divisions. Send us your Spirit to lead to full unity and your sons and daughters in full charity, in obedience to your will, through Christ our Lord. Amen.

(General Audience during the
Week of Prayer for Christian Unity,
21.1.81—OR, 26.1.81)

FOR VOCATIONS

54. Lord Jesus, who called those you wanted to call, call many
of us to work for you, to work with you.

You, who enlightened with your words those whom
you called, enlighten us with faith in you.

You, who supported them in their difficulties, help us
to conquer the difficulties we have as young people today.

And if you call one of us to be consecrated completely
to you, may your love give warmth to this vocation from
its very beginning and make it grow and persevere to the
end.   Amen.

(From the Pope's Message for the
16th World Day of Prayer
for Vocations,
1979—OR, 30.4.79)

55. Let us all pray with the Blessed Virgin, trusting in her
intercession. Let us pray that the most holy mysteries of the
Risen Christ and of the Spirit, the Paraclete, may enlighten
many generous people, ready to serve the Church with
greater readiness. Let us pray for the pastors and their
collaborators, that they may find the right words in putting
before the faithful the message of the priestly and
consecrated life. Let us pray that in all parts of the Church
the faithful may believe with renewed fervour in the Gospel
ideal of the priest completely dedicated to the building up
of the kingdom of God: and let us pray that they support
such vocations with generosity. Let us pray for the young
people, to whom the Lord extends his invitation to follow
him more closely, that they may not be drawn away by the
things of this world, but may open their hearts to the loving
voice that is calling them; let us pray that they may feel
capable of dedicating themselves for their whole lives, "with
undivided heart", to Christ, the Church and souls; let
us pray that they may believe that grace gives them the

strength to make this gift, and that they may see the beauty and greatness of the priestly, religious and missionary life. Let us pray for families, that they may succeed in creating a Christian environment favourable to the important religious choices of their children. And at the same time with all our hearts let us thank the Lord that in these recent years, in many parts of the world, many young and not so young people are responding in growing numbers to the divine call. Let us pray that all priests and religious may be and example and an encouragement to those who have been called, by their availability and humble readiness— as I said in my letter to priests on Holy Thursday 1979— "to accept the gifts of the Holy Spirit and to transmit to others the fruits of love and peace, to give them that certainty of faith from which derive the profound understanding of the meaning of human existence and the capacity to introduce the moral order into the life of individuals and of the human setting."

(From the Pope's Message for the
17th World Day of Prayer
for Vocations,
1980—OR, 14.1.80)

56. May each local Church hear in these words of mine a fresh invitation from Christ to pray the Lord of the harvest "to send labourers into his harvest" (Mt 9 : 38; Lk 10 : 2). And so, dear brothers and sons and daughters, let us join in a prayer as wide as the world, as strong as our faith, as persevering as the love that the Holy Spirit has poured out into our hearts; through this prayer,

—*let us praise the Lord,* who has enriched his Church with the gift of the priesthood, with the many different forms of consecrated life and with numberless other graces, for the building up of his people and for the service of humanity;

—*let us give thanks to the Lord,* who continues to send out his call, to which many young people and others, in these years and in various parts of the world, are responding with growing generosity;

—*let us ask pardon of the Lord* for our weaknesses and infidelities, which perhaps discourage others from responding to his call;

—*let us fervently ask the Lord* to grant to pastors, to religious, to missionaries and other consecrated persons the gifts of wisdom, counsel and prudence in calling others to the total service of God and the Church; may he also grant to ever more numerous young people and others not so young the generosity and courage to respond and to persevere.

Let us all offer this humble and trusting prayer, entrusting it to the intercession of Mary, Mother of the Church, Queen of the clergy, the shining model for every person consecrated to the service of the people of God.

(From the Pope's Message for the
18th World Day of Prayer
for Vocations,
1981—OR, 27.4.81)

FOR WORKERS

57. Dearly beloved brothers and sisters in Christ: the Pope invites you to pray with him and with the universal Church, so that all the farmers and workers of the world will live their dignity, fulfil their role worthily and make their great contribution to the building up of the kingdom of Christ, for the glory of the Most Holy Trinity. And may Our Lady of Penafrancia continue to love you, console you, and protect you and your families and your country.   Amen.

(Legazpi City, Penaranda Park, Philippines,
21.2.81—OR, 2.3.81)

58. I pray to God ardently for the happiness of all:
—that your just aspirations may be realized;
—that the moments and the reasons of crisis may be overcome;
—that work will never be an alienation for anyone;
—that, on the contrary, it may be honoured by everyone as it deserves, so that justice and even more love may triumph in it;
—that the environment of work will really be fit for man, and that man may be able to appreciate it as an extension of his own family;
—that work may help man to be more of a man;
—and that, with the commitment of everyone, it may be possible to arrive at the construction of a new society and a new world, in the full realization of justice, freedom and peace.

(Pope's address to the workers of
Terni, Italy,
19.3.81—OR, 30.3.81)

FOR THOSE WORKING WITH
THE MASS MEDIA

59. I earnestly invite all media workers to join us in the Church's
day of reflection and prayer. We beg the Almighty together
to deepen their consciousness of the tremendous opportunity
which is theirs to serve mankind and to shape the world
towards good. We ask him to endow them with the understanding, wisdom and courage which they will always
need in bearing their awesome responsibility. We beg him to
keep them always intensely mindful of their audiences,
which for the most part are families like their own, with
overworked parents often too tired to be alert, and with
children who are trusting, impressionable, vulnerable and
easily led. For remembering this they will keep in mind
also the enormous consequences which their work may
have for good or ill and will not easily be false to themselves
or to the principles of their noble calling.

(From the Pope's Message for
World Communications Day,
1980—OR, 19.5.80)

FOR THE DEAD

60. The eight Beatitudes are the Gospel code of holiness, by which all those whom the Church remembers today with such veneration and love were inspired and to which they remained faithful up to the end.

For all our brothers and sisters who rest in this Verano Cemetery and in all the graveyards of Rome and of the world, may the words of Christ in the Sermon on the Mount become the Good News of eternal salvation.

May the kingdom of heaven be theirs.

May they possess it as a "Promised Land".

May they have eternal joy.

May they be satisfied in their hunger and thirst for righteousness.

May they be called children of God for ever.

May they see God face to face.

May their joy and happiness be full and unlimited.

Let us pray: "O God, the glory of believers and the life of the just, who saved us by the death and resurrection of your Son, be merciful to our deceased brothers and sisters. When they were in our midst they professed faith in the resurrection; give them endless bliss. Through Christ our Lord".

(At the Verano Cemetery, Rome,
1.11.81—OR, 9.11.81)

TO THE MERCIFUL LOVE

61. Merciful Love, we pray to you, do not fail!
Merciful Love, be tireless!
Be constantly greater than every evil, which is in man
and in the world. Be greater than that evil which has
increased in our century and in our generation!
Be more powerful with the power of the crucified King!
"Blessed be his kingdom which is coming".

(At the Shrine of Merciful Love,
Collevalenza,
22.11.81—OR, 30.11.81)

GLORY TO CHRIST, THE WORD OF GOD

62. Glory to you, O Christ, the Word of God.

Glory to you every day in this blessed period of Lent.

Glory to you today, the day of the Lord and the fifth Sunday of this period.

Glory to you, Word of God, who became flesh and manifested yourself with your life and carried out your mission on earth with your death and resurrection.

Glory to you, Word of God, who penetrate the recesses of human hearts, and show them the way of salvation.

Glory to you in every place on earth.

Glory to you in this peninsula between the peaks of the Alps and the Mediterranean. Glory to you in all the places of this blessed region: glory to you in every city and village, the inhabitants of which have been listening to you and walking in your light for nearly two thousand years.

Glory to you, Word of God, Word of Lent, which is the time of our salvation, of mercy and repentance.

Glory to you for an illustrious son of this land.

Glory to you, Word of God, whom a son of this land— known to the whole Church and to the world by the name of Benedict—listened to for the first time here, in this place called Norcia, and accepted as the light of his own life, and also of that of his brothers and sisters.

Word of God that will never pass away, one thousand five hundred years have now passed since the birth of Benedict, your confessor and monk, the Founder of the Order, the Patriarch of the West, the Patron Saint of Europe.

Glory to you, Word of God.

(Norcia, 23.3.80—OR, 31.3.80)

VARIOUS

63. We wait for the moment of Christ's new birth in the liturgy, for he is the one who "instructs sinners in the way" (Ps 25 : 8-9).

And so we turn will full confidence and conviction towards the one who will come—towards Christ. And we say to him: Lead! Lead me in truth! Lead us in truth!

Lead in truth, O Christ, the fathers and mothers of families in the parish. Urged on and strengthened by the sacramental grace of marriage and aware of being on earth visible sign of your unfailing love for the Church, let them be serene and firm in shouldering with evangelical consistency the responsibility of married life and of the Christian upbringing of their children.

Lead in truth, O Christ, the young of the parish. Let them not be attracted by the new idols, such as exaggerated consumerism, prosperity at all costs, moral permissiveness, protest expressed with violence, but live with joy your message, which is the message of the Beatitudes, the message of love for God and one's neighbour, the message of moral commitment for the real transformation of society.

Lead in truth, O Christ, all the faithful of the parish. May Christian faith animate their whole life and make them become, before the world, courageous witnesses to your mission of salvation, responsible and dynamic members of the Church, happy to be sons of God and brothers, with you, of all men!

Lead us in truth, O Christ! Always!

(Church of St Clement, Rome,
2.12.79—OR, 24.12.79)

64. May spouses pray for the grace of perseverance in conjugal faithfulness and in that of parents. May they pray to obtain the love necessary to carry out the vocation they have received from God.

May children find in this parish a vaster family home; may they absorb in catechesis the truth of the word of God; may they be nourished with the Body of the Saviour.

May the young seek in this parish support for their ideals and commit themselves to animating with their new life, with their witness, with readiness to serve God and man.

May the sick and the suffering find consolation and relief here. May Christ visit them, by means of the service of the priests, and explain to them with the interior word of the Spirit the great dignity and significance of their sufferings.

May all, in this parish, become aware of being members of the Body of Christ and realize that the Kingdom of God is approaching them, that, in fact, it is already present in them.

I pray for all these today, together with you, trusting above all in the intercession of Mary, who is Mother of the Church and the Cause of our Joy.

(Church of St Raphael, Rome,
11.11.79—OR, 17.12.79)

65. Blessed be the Lord
who prolongs in this way his work among us!
May all the Apostles intercede for us!
May the Virgin Mary,
    the Mother of our Saviour,
    the Mother of the Church,
    the Queen of Apostles,
intercede for us!
We dedicate to her
these new servants of the Church.
Let us give thanks to the Lord,
in faith, and charity, and hope!
Amen.   Alleluia!

(Kinshasa, 4.5.80—OR, 19.5.80)

66. O Mother of our Advent,
be with us and see to it
that he will remain with us
in this difficult Advent
of the struggles for truth and hope,
for justice and peace:
He, alone, Emmanuel!

(Basilica of St Mary Major, Rome,
8.12.79—OR, 7.1.80)

67. God has shown his own pleasure in man!
God is pleased with man.
The people awake; man arises;
"the shepherd of his destiny is awakened".
How often man is crushed by this destiny.
How often he is its prisoner.
How often he dies of hunger, is near despair,
is threatened in the awareness
of the meaning of his own humanity.
How often, in spite of all
the appearances he creates,
man is far from being pleased with himself.
But today he awakes
and hears the proclamation:
God is born into human history!
God is pleased with man.
God has become man.
God is pleased with you!   Amen.

(Basilica of St Peter, Rome,
Homily at Midnight Mass,
24.12.79—OR, 14.1.80)

68. May Christmas find each of us
engaged in rediscovering the message
that comes from the manger in Bethlehem.
A little courage is necessary,
but it is worthwhile,

because only if we can open out in this way
to the coming of Christ,
will we be able to experience
the peace announced by the Angels
during that holy night.
May Christmas be for you all
a meeting with Christ,
who became man to give every man
the capacity of becoming a son of God.

(Audience, 23.12.81—OR, 4.1.82)

69. May Light come,
and illuminate the darkness
of human existence,
even the most difficult one.
May Grace come,
and reveal the dignity of mankind,
which is derived from the mystery
of the Birth of God.
May every man arise
from whatever depression he labours under.
"Alma Redemptoris Mater! Succurre! " . . .
May the prayer of the Church
and of all men of goodwill
surround Poland, my native land:
"Alma Redemptoris Mater . . .
succurre cadenti, surgere qui curat populo! "

("Angelus" Message,
20.12.81—OR, 4.1.82)

70. "The right hand of the Lord is exalted,
the right hand of the Lord does valiantly.
I shall not die, but I shall live,
and recount the deeds of the Lord (Ps 117/118: 16-17).
Christ, the Son of the living God,
accept from us this holy vigil on Easter night
and give us that joy of the new Life,

which we bear within us,
which only you can give to the human heart:
You, the Risen Christ,
You, our paschal Lamb!

(Basilica of St Peter, Rome,
Homily, Easter Vigil,
5.4.80—OR, 14.4.80)

71. May the Holy Spirit,
The Spirit of Pentecost,
help you to clarify what is ambiguous,
to give warmth to what is indifferent,
to enlighten what is obscure,
to be before the world true and
generous witnesses of Christ's love,
for "no one can live without love".

(Institute Catholique, Paris,
1.6.80—OR, 16.6.80)

72. Here we are
in the Year of the Lord 1982!
"To him belong time and the centuries.
To him be glory and power
for ever and ever." (Liturgy of Holy Saturday)
Besides greeting you,
dear brothers and sisters,
I greet the new year,
above all by glorifying God
who alone is eternal,
unlimited in time.
He alone is Truth and Love.
He is Omnipotence and Mercy.
He alone is Holy.
He is the One who is.
He is the Father, Son and Holy Spirit
in the absolute Unity of the Divinity.
So I greet this new year
together with you

in the Name of our Lord Jesus Christ:
there is, in fact, no other Name
in which we could be saved.
In the Name of Jesus Christ
I embrace this year,
that it may be a time of salvation
for the Church and for the world.
In the Name of Jesus Christ
I say to this year:
"The Lord bless and keep you.
The Lord make his face to shine upon you,
and be gracious to you.
The Lord lift up his countenance upon you,
and give you his peace" (Num 6:24.26).

("Angelus" Message,
1.1.82—OR, 11.1.82)

◇

May all find their dwelling in thee, O Lord.
Next May I will make an apostolic pilgrimage to
Great Britain to strengthen (cf. Lk 22:32) our brothers
in the episcopate and the sons and daughters of the
Catholic dioceses of that noble land. On this occasion
I will also meet the Archbishop of Canterbury and
Primate of the Anglican Communion, Dr Robert Runcie.

May this journey of mine also serve the cause
of the rapport between the Catholic Church and the
Anglican Communion, and hasten the greatly desired
union. For this end, which is of great importance,
I ask you all for fervent prayers to the Holy Trinity.

May St Paul, through the merits of his glorious
martyrdom, grant that all we believers in Jesus may
"attain to the unity of the faith and of the knowledge
of the Son of God, to mature manhood, to the measure
of the stature of the fullness of Christ" (Eph 4:12f).

("Angelus" Message,
17.1.82—OR, 25.1.82)

◇

INDEX

(The number is that of the prayer given in the text)

Accra 26
Adalbert, St 44
Advent 66
Africa 26
Albert the Great, St 39
Altötting 25
Asia 27
Austria 25
Baclaran 2, 27
Baltimore 18
Beatitudes 60, 63
Benedict XIV 34
Benedict, St 32, 62
Boniface, St 25
Brazil 21, 28, 43
Chad 30
Christ Child 34
Christ Redeemer 5, 6, 7
Christ the Word 62
Christian Unity 12, 18, 25, 50, 51, 52, 53
Christmas 67, 68, 69
Clemente, Basilica of San 40, 63
Collevalenza 61
Cologne 39
Colosseum 5, 6, 7
Congo 30
Consolata, Basilica of 49
Consolation 49
Cyril and Methodius, Sts 41
Dante 23
Dead 61
de Marillac, St Louise 24
de Solminihac, Bl Alain 45
Easter 70
Elizabeth, St 24
El Salvador 15
Eucharist 8, 9, 10
Europe 25, 32, 36, 40
Evangelization 21, 27, 34
Family 19, 20, 46
Fortaleza 28
Frascati 22

Francis of Assisi, St 41
Gabriel the Archangel 14
Germany 25, 39
Ghana 26
God the Father 3
Good Friday 5, 6, 7
Guadalupe 19, 34
Hiroshima 48
Holy Spirit 11, 12, 13, 20, 21, 24, 25, 26, 28, 34, 39, 46, 71
Homeless 4
Immaculate Conception 14, 15, 16, 17, 18, 19
Ireland 31
Italy 33
Japan 33
Jasna Gora 20, 29, 36, 44, 50
Joseph, St 42
John Paul II 1, 2 etc
Kinshasa 37
Kisangani 38
Knock 31
Kolbe, Bl Maximilian 24, 33
Laboure', St Catherine 24
Latin America 34
Legazpi 18
Lent 62
Lourdes 9
Mary Major, Basilica of St 12
Mary, Motherhood of 12
Mary, Mother of the Church 2, 12, 19, 20 etc
Martyrs 2, 38
Mass media 59
May, month of 23
Merciful Love 61
Mexico 19, 34
Miraculous Medal, Chapel of 24
Missionaries 30, 37, 38
Nagasaki 33
Norcia 32, 62
New Year 72
Our Lady Aparecida 28, 29

Pampuri, Bl Riccardo 45
Paris 24, 71
Parish 63, 64
Paul, St 15 ,43
Peace 29, 30, 32, 39, 47, 48
Pentecost 11, 12, 71
Peter, St 15, 25, 30, 43
Peter, Basilica of St 10
Philippines 27
Pius IX 14
Pius X, St 34
Pius XII 14
Poland 15, 20, 35, 36, 41, 44, 69
Raphael, Church of St 64

Repetto, Bl Maria 45
Scrosoppi, Bl Luigi 45
Stanislaus, St 44
Terni 58
Thevenet, Bl Claudine 45
"Totus tuus" 24, 29, 36
USA 18
Verano 60
Violence 15, 32
Vocations 19, 20, 24, 49, 54, 55, 56, 57, 58
Workers 57, 58
Zaïre 37